CRAVE
WASHINGTON DC

The Urban Girl's Manifesto

Melody Biringer

the urban girl
manifes

The Urban Girl's Manifesto

We CRAVE Community.

At CRAVE DC we believe in acknowledging, celebrating, and passionately supporting local businesses. We know that, when encouraged to thrive, neighborhood establishments enhance communities and provide rich experiences not usually encountered in mass-market. By introducing you to the savvy businesswomen in this guide, we hope that CRAVE DC will help inspire your own inner entrepreneur.

We CRAVE Adventure.

We could all use a getaway, and at CRAVE DC we believe that you don't need to be a jet-setter to have a little adventure. There's so much to do and explore right in your own backyard. We encourage you to break your routine, to venture away from your regular haunts, to visit new businesses, to explore all the funky finds and surprising spots that DC has to offer. Whether it's to hunt for a birthday gift, indulge in a spa treatment, order a bouquet of flowers, or connect with like-minded people, let CRAVE DC be your guide for a one-of-a-kind hometown adventure.

We CRAVE Quality.

CRAVE DC is all about quality products and thoughtful service. We know that a satisfying shopping trip requires more than a simple exchange of money for goods, and that a rejuvenating spa date entails more than a quick clip of the cuticles and a swipe of polish. We know you want to come away feeling uplifted, beautiful, excited, relaxed, relieved and, above all, knowing you got the most bang for your buck. We have scoured the city to find the hidden gems, new hot spots, and old standbys, all with one thing in common: they're the best of the best!

A Guide to Our Guide

CRAVE DC is more than a guidebook. It's a savvy, quality-of-lifestyle book devoted entirely to the best local businesses owned by women. CRAVE DC will direct you to more than 100 local spots—top boutiques, spas, cafés, stylists, fitness studios, and more. And we'll introduce you to the inspired, dedicated women behind these exceptional enterprises, for whom creativity, quality, innovation, and customer service are paramount. Not only is CRAVE DC an intelligent guidebook for those wanting to know what's happening throughout town, it's a directory for those who value the contributions that spirited businesswomen make to our city.

CRAVE Categories

 Abode Furniture, home improvement, and interior design

 Adorn Jewelry, eyewear, handbags, and accessories

 Children's Goods and services for babies, children, and parents

 Connect Networking, media, technology, and event services

 Details Gifts, books, small home accessories, florists, and stationery

 Enhance Beauty, wellness, spas, and fitness

 Escape Entertainment, travel, and leisure activities

 Pets Goods and services for pets and their owners

 Sip Savor Food and drink

 Style Clothing, shoes, and stylists

 Sustainable Devoted to environmentally friendly practices

 Nonprofit Not-for-profit business

 Discount Offers a discount in Craving Savings

Table of Contents

Featured Entreprenesses

*Including retailers, restaurants,
fitness studios, fashion designers,
online retailers, event planners, home
accessories, pet stores, lifestyle
and wellness-related products,
travel services, spas, and salons.*

3GREENMOMS

800.443.2302
lunchskins.com, Twitter: @3greenmoms

Modern. Simple. Green.

3greenmoms are the local inventors of super stylish, eco-friendly LunchSkins.
These cheerful, reusable, food-safe fabric bags have changed the way people
bring lunches to work and school. In just the first year of sales, LunchSkins
saved more than 12 million plastic bags from landfills and waterways.

Kirsten Quigley and Cris Bourelly

 # Q&A

What are your most popular products or services?
LunchSkins sandwich size-reusable bags—right now, the red apples and polka dot patterns are big hits.

What or who inspired you to start your business?
20 million sandwich bags are thrown away each day in the United States. We want to change that.

Who is your role model or mentor?
We come from families of entrepreneurs, with backgrounds in art, engineering, and real estate—so we grew up exposed to the ins and outs of business.

How do you spend your free time?
Outside! On bikes, in the garden, hiking, skiing, and enjoying family and friends.

Ann Sullivan

Q&A

What are your most popular products or services?
Custom-designed embroidered linens, our bridal registry, and "the perfect gift" for the hostess who has everything!

People may be surprised to know...
Opening Abrielle was my MBA thesis.

What or who inspired you to start your business?
My passion for beautiful linens.

How do you spend your free time?
Traveling with family and friends, attending the ballet and theater, and going to museums.

What is your indulgence?
The perfect cappuccino, and getting seaside spa treatments.

ABRIELLE FINE
LINENS AND LINGERIE

3301 New Mexico Ave NW, Washington, 202.364.6118

Luxurious. Timeless. Unique.
Abrielle is a fine linen and lingerie boutique, celebrating their 25th year in business. They offer an extensive collection of the finest European linens and hand embroideries, as well as beautiful, yet comfortable, sleepwear. They are known for their personalized service, specializing in custom designs and sized linens for bed, bath, table, and baby. Every lifestyle needs a little romance!

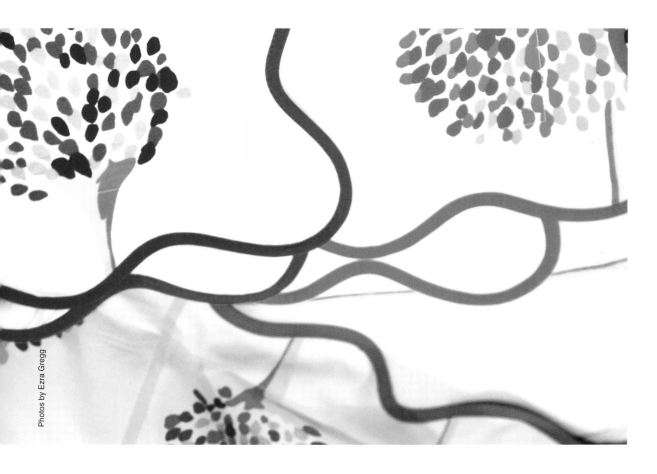

Photos by Ezra Gregg

Meagan Kurtz

 # Q&A

What are your most popular products or services?
ADMK Jewelry's simple, yet elegant earrings and necklaces that combine unusual shapes and bold colors.

People may be surprised to know...
I don't wear much elaborate jewelry on a daily basis. My daily wardrobe consists of jeans, sweatpants and T-shirts—so the occasion to get dressed up is a nice treat!

What business mistake have you made that you will not repeat?
Not walking the floor of trade shows before exhibiting.

What do you CRAVE? In business? In life?
The ability to take one day at a time in life, love, business, and success.

ADMK JEWELRY

$

571.243.6127
admkjewelry.com, Twitter: @admkjewelry.com

Stylish. Elegant. Chic.

ADMK (Adorn Designs by Meagan Kurtz) Jewelry is handcrafted, distinctive jewelry made from the highest quality cultured freshwater pearls, cubic zirconia, Swarovski crystals, semi-precious gemstones, and precious metals. ADMK Jewelry combines the natural beauty of gemstones with a bit of flair, offering a stylish and sophisticated complement to any outfit.

AFFINITY LAB

2451 18th St NW, Washington, 202.518.6181
920 U St NW, Washington, 202.332.1360
affinitylab.com, Twitter: @affinitylab

Creative. Innovative. Green.
Affinity Lab is shared office space for small businesses, entrepreneurs,
and nonprofits. The Lab provides office space and business tools,
but it is the business community of other like-minded owners,
artists, and creatives that makes membership valuable.

Photos by Patrick Onofre Photography, except portrait by Karen Leonard

Berit Oskey

Q&A

What or who inspired you to start your business?
My business partners and I were entrepreneurs
who first started a web development
business; we saw the need for shared
office space and a supportive business
community so we created it ourselves.

People may be surprised to know...
We've been open for more than nine years
and our Adams Morgan location was the
first coworking space in the country.

Who is your role model or mentor?
Gloria Steinem is a role model for me.
In her recent writings and lectures she's
stressed the importance of supporting
women in all roles, including child care.
She's always been a hard worker.

Adams Morgan

U Street

ANGELA SPICER
ECO MAKE UP ARTIST

Located at The Still Point: 1 Columbia Ave, Takoma Park, 301.920.0801
Available for freelance in the Washington DC area: 240.601.6140
angelaspicer.com, Twitter: @synergy_makeup

Healthy. Vibrant. Transformative.
Angela Spicer is a talented, professional make-up artist. She has been
creating beautiful looks for brides, actors, entertainers, and models for
more than 25 years. She specializes in eco-friendly and organic makeup.
She gives individual makeup lessons and makes sure her clients have the
tools, techniques, and practice to recreate their application at home.

Angela Spicer

Q&A

What or who inspired you to start your business?
Being happy every time I do makeup
made me realize that I'll always be
making my living this way!

People may be surprised to know...
I used to be a photographer. My speciality
was black-and-white sepia-toned prints.

Who is your role model or mentor?
Sara Damelio, owner of Skincando, inspired me
to use organic, eco-makeup exclusively. Also
my parents, who are kind and hard-working.

How do you spend your free time?
Playing with my 5-year-old daughter is such
fun and keeps me fit! I also enjoy reading,
listening to music, and eating out.

What do you CRAVE? In business? In life?
Connections with like-minded
people, and creativity... always!

Jenet Ahn

Q&A

People may be surprised to know...
Annalee's carries gowns in 00 to plus
sizes; we register each gown to each
event to avoid duplications!

What or who inspired you to start your business?
My aunt, who has been in this business
for almost 30 years, and myself—I
always wanted to wear beautiful gowns
to attend social functions in DC!

Who is your role model or mentor?
Rosemary Tran Lauer (Devotion to Children).
Against all odds this single mom, who fled
Vietnam in 1975 with little English, rose to
the top of not one, but two professions.

What is your indulgence?
Listening to various instrumental versions
of Pachelbel's "Canon in D Major" with a
cup of cappuccino and crème brûlée.

ANNALEE'S
PROM, BRIDAL, &
SPECIAL OCCASIONS

42395 Ryan Road, Ste 104, Ashburn, 703.722.2588
annaleesformals.com

Elegant. Glamorous. Stylish.
Women of all ages want to look and feel pretty, radiant, unique, and
even sexy! It is mandatory to look our absolute best at a formal event.
And don't we love a special occasion as an opportunity to pull out the
stops and look divine. Annalee's is one of the premier resources in the
Washington DC metropolitan area for formal and bridal gowns.

APRÈS PEAU

1430 K St NW, Washington, 202.783.0022
aprespeau.com, Twitter: @aprespeau

Unique. Modern. Apropos.
DC trendsetters flock to Après Peau for the curated collection of original and stylish luxuries. Created to make the experience of finding that apropos gift (for yourself and others) easy and fun, Après Peau features an ever-evolving sampling of must-haves. Each product is hand-selected for its smart, unique, practical, or entertaining commentary on living and giving in Washington.

 # Q&A

What are your most popular products or services?
Hard-to-find diffusers, candles, and unique letterpress stationery. For the DC enthusiast, our award-winning Washington-themed chocolate bars are a must!

People may be surprised to know...
Après Peau is French for "after skin." I am the founding director of the Washington Institute of Dermatologic Laser Surgery and a clinical professor of dermatology at Georgetown University. In my opinion, our skin is our ultimate accessory. After skin, there is Après Peau!

How do you spend your free time?
Traveling with family and friends. I am always on the lookout for unique gifts to sell at Après Peau.

What is your indulgence?
A week in Europe with my family every year.

Tina Alster

ART BY CHOCOLATE

202.328.1935
artbychocolate.com, Twitter: @chocolateartist

Unique. Delicious. Exquisite.
Art By Chocolate is a boutique gourmet chocolate company specializing in hand-rendered flowers and leaves in custom-blended colors. They offer clients an interactive chocolate-ordering experience unlike any other company! LolliChocs, Luscious Leaves, and Precious Petals make up arrangements, bouquets, and gift boxes perfect for every occasion.

Photos by Patrick Onofre Photography

Lee Reizian Holmes

Q&A

What or who inspired you to start your business?
I made a list of some of my favorite things—
flowers, chocolate, and painting—and
then designed my business around those
things! What better way to make a living
than spending time doing what you love?

**What business mistake have you
made that you will not repeat?**
I was a bit timid at first, but I've
since learned to be fearless!

People may be surprised to know...
I started my career as a singer and
TV commercial producer.

**Where is your favorite place to
go with your girlfriends?**
We like to explore many places—
especially those offering good red wine
and delicious food, and is quiet so that
we can chat to our hearts' content!

Judith Leary Harkins
and Shannon Denny-Price

Q&A

What are your most popular
products or services?
Earrings are a specialty, with thousands
of pairs in a wide variety of styles and
materials, including clip-ons.

What or who inspired you to start your business?
We met in a craft co-op and felt the
need to find a better retail environment
to promote local craft artists.

What business mistake have you
made that you will not repeat?
Not anticipating how even minor
staffing changes affect everyone.

How do you spend your free time?
Gardening and being outside
as much as possible.

THE ARTISANS

1368 Chain Bridge Road, McLean, 703.506.0158
theartisansblog.biz

Artsy. Handmade. Colorful.

The Artisans is a fun, fabulous, and funky gift store with 20 years of experience making customers happy. The boutique features artsy, colorful gifts, jewelry, accessories, clothing, pottery, glass, home and garden accents, and more. Many items are handmade, either around the corner by local artisans, or around the world by fair-trade artisans.

Photos by Meredith Rizzo Photography

Audrey Johnson

Q&A

What or who inspired you to start your business?
I have always wanted to have my own business. As a busy professional, I did not have time to do the tasks required in my personal life to keep organized, and plan for travel or other activities that were important to me. I thought it would be great if I had "someone" who knew me well enough to think about these things and take care of the details while I focus on work and other activities. I knew there had to be others who needed that "someone" to help them, too!

What do you CRAVE? In business? In life?
In business, inspiring and empowering my clients to simplify their lives and enhance their experiences, ultimately helping them to live their best life. In life, success, good times, more shoes, work-life balance, perfect health, and never-ending opportunities to help others be successful.

 AUDREYLYNNJO LLC

202.384.4890
audreylynnjo.com, Twitter: @AudreyLynnJo

Exclusive. Personalized. Resourceful.
AudreyLynnJo LLC is a premier concierge and lifestyle management company, offering all-inclusive lifestyle solutions to a distinguished few, who require uncommon regular arrangements due to their hectic schedules, noteworthy professions, and demanding societal expectations. Audrey presents a style of living to her clients that allows them to focus on the activities that are most important and enjoyable.

BARDANGLE JEWELRY

202.744.8099
bardangle.com

Stylish. Wearable. Affordable.

Bardangle Jewelry works with designers and artisans from all over the world to bring you unique jewelry and fashion accessories. Bardangle Jewelry celebrates only the highest standard in quality, design, and craftsmanship. In addition, the uniquely shaped bags and scarves are purchased from villages throughout Southeast Asia and are made of 100 percent pure silk. Bardangle continues to grow through its Independent Sales Associate program.

Photos by Patrick Onofre Photography, except portrait by Maggie Winters. Main photo (this page) and top middle photo (opposite page) taken at the Arthur M. Sackler Gallery at the Smithsonian Institution

Barbara Kinney

Q&A

What are your most popular products or services?
Our colorful 100 percent silk bags and scarves are distinctive to Bardangle Jewelry. Our most popular is the foldable square bag.

What business mistake have you made that you will not repeat?
I didn't keep accurate records of inventory. I learned the hard way that good records are key to a successful business.

How do you spend your free time?
Shopping! Or else, I plan... whether it's a trip, a meal, or a day's outing, I'm always researching something.

What is your indulgence?
I am an avid traveler and am always seeking out my next adventure.

BLISSLIVING HOME

866.952.5477
blisslivinghome.com, Twitter: @blissliving

Global. Modern. Stylish.
Established in 2007, Blissliving Home is the destination interior lifestyle brand
for the stylish consumer seeking modern design with global influences.
Inspired by creator and CEO Mei Xu's passion for travel, contemporary
art, fashion, and design, every collection is an invitation to experience
the excitement of travel, the rush of adventure, and the exploration
of world cultures through design, texture, color, and fragrance.

Mei Xu

Q&A

What are your most popular products or services?
Bedding, decorative pillows, throw blankets, home décor pieces, candles, home fragrance, bathroom accessories, shower curtains, and wall art.

What or who inspired you to start your business?
The many hotel rooms I have stayed in over the years that lacked inspiring design elements or sumptuous, soft bedding.

How do you spend your free time?
I enjoy time with family and friends, practice yoga, and visit plenty of art exhibitions.

Where is your favorite place to go with your girlfriends?
It's the company that counts, not the place. Any place can be the best place when I am with my girlfriends!

Kelly Bradley

Q&A

What or who inspired you to start your business?
Living a healthy lifestyle gives me the energy to live my best life ever. I want others to experience this, too.

People may be surprised to know...
I love modern green architecture and design, mid-century modern decor, and photography.

What business mistake have you made that you will not repeat?
Taking on too much at one time!

What is your indulgence?
I love indulging in big bowls of my homemade raw ice cream. Yummy!

What do you CRAVE? In business? In life?
Living in the moment and making the most out of every day.

BRADLEY WELLNESS

$

202.320.5025
bradleywellness.com

Fresh. Vibrant. Empowering.
Bradley Wellness provides a variety of services dedicated to healthy living including nutrition and health coaching, juice cleansing programs, raw living food preparation classes, wellness workshops and retreats, corporate wellness programs, yoga, therapeutic Pilates and gyrotonic exercise, and physical therapy.

THE CALPRO GROUP ✆

1717 N St NW, Washington, 240.888.9494
thecalprogroup.com

Cutting-edge. Creative. Innovative.
The CALPRO Group (TCG) provides services in designing, managing, planning, and operating a host of various types of events/trade shows. TCG also works closely with an array of general contractors and vendors who service any type of event. Their extensive knowledge of numerous venues in cities across the United States and Canada allows them to assist you in locating and negotiating the best value.

Sydney B. Williams

Q&A

People may be surprised to know...
The CALPRO Group does events all over
the country as well as in Canada.

What or who inspired you to start your business?
Wanting to create my own opportunities
to be my own boss and not be
confined to a 9–5 mentality.

How do you spend your free time?
With the very little free time that I have, I
enjoy being outdoors, taking beach vacations,
and spending time with family and friends.

What do you CRAVE? In business? In life?
I crave waking up every day excited to take
on new challenges, creating an amazing
experience for my clients, and helping
to create opportunities for others.

Dupont Circle

Abrielle Fine Linens and Lingerie
photographed by Ezra Gregg

What business mistake have you
made that you will not repeat?

*"Not stopping to smell the roses.
I've learned the importance
of pausing, celebrating, and
expressing gratitude."*

Terri Holley of Creative Blog Solutions

CANDY BEADS JEWELRY

202.360.7086
candybeadsjewelry.com

Elegant. Colorful. Unique.

Only the best quality gems in cut, vibrant color, and shimmering polish are used in owner Beth Rosenheim's work. She specializes in finding unique fantasy-cut gemstones to design and craft exclusive and classic jewelry. Candy Beads Jewelry fits gracefully into a woman's day-to-day lifestyle with easy-to-wear elegance.

Photos by Patrick Onofre Photography

Beth Rosenheim

Q&A

What or who inspired you to start your business?
I've made jewelry since I was in college,
but gave it up when my children were
born. I didn't realize how much I missed
the creative outlet until a girlfriend
encouraged me to pick it up again.

People may be surprised to know...
My work is very successful at the fine
jewelry store Tiny Jewel Box downtown.

Who is your role model or mentor?
Alex Sepkus's exquisite and intricate wax
carving, use of fine gemstones, and ability
to be a successful artist and businessman
have inspired me and my work.

How do you spend your free time?
Walking and enjoying nature's beauty
around Widewater at Great Falls with
my family on the weekends.

Carla David

# Q&A

What or who inspired you to start your business?
When I was in the fifth grade, my best friend
and I hand-stamped pieces of paper and sold
the "stationery" to our neighbors to make money
for summer camp. That started a passion
for all things paper. Now the fire is burning
full-force in my full-service design studio.

People may be surprised to know...
The invitation to your event doesn't
have to be a rectangular piece of paper.
We truly can design anything the mind
can imagine. The sky's the limit!

How do you spend your free time?
If I'm not with family and friends, you'll
find me in the kitchen, baking up a storm,
or packing my bags and traveling.

CARLA DAVID DESIGN

301.300.5996
carladaviddesign.com, Twitter: @couturedesigns

Couture. Creative. Personal.
Carla David Design is a graphic design boutique specializing in custom, handcrafted, couture invitations for life's special moments. They start the party with extraordinarily clean, elegant designs and the finest printing techniques. From wedding invitations, baby announcements, save-the-dates, and holiday cards to menu cards, favors, and personal stationery, they design the details that make your event, wedding, and life charming and fun.

Photos by Troy o Ex Voto Studio

CATALYST GOURMET & GIFTS

888.229.0212
catalystgourmet.com, Twitter: @catalystmom

Elegant. Innovative. Delicious.
Catalyst Gourmet handcrafts innovative products using all-natural,
gluten-free, beneficial spices to support healthy living and wellness.
They transform the taste of tea, coffee, and more—enjoy Catalyst Tea
Enhancers, Creative Curries, Gourmet Finishing Sugars, or Baked Bites
of Bliss. Catalyst Gourmet also caters fabulous tea and dessert parties,
creates custom gift baskets, and offers private cooking seminars.

Photos by Gunnar Larson

Kaushika Patel

Q&A

What or who inspired you to start your business?
I was an IVF mom on bed-rest, drinking a cup of green tea, when the idea for Catalyst Tea Enhancers was born. With a family history of diabetes and strokes, I decided to create gourmet products that transform ordinary beverages and foods to make healthy living more flavorful and fun.

People may be surprised to know...
I love to paint. Catalyst Gourmet's labels and stationery feature my own original works of art.

Who is your role model or mentor?
My parents taught us to work hard and play hard. Every life milestone was celebrated in a big way with amazing food and a sense of community, creativity, and joy.

What do you CRAVE? In business? In life?
Being a positive catalyst—I want to enable others to be joyful, creative, confident, and healthy.

CELEBRATING YOU THE SPA

800.399.9557
celebratingyou.com, Twitter: @celebratingu

Luxurious. Rejuvenating. Soothing.
Celebrating You provides upscale premium on-site spa services. Designed for the cultivated consumer who prefers the repose of a spa in the privacy and comfort of their surroundings, Celebrating You offers the ultimate spa experience. From perfect pedicures and manicures to signature facials and rejuvenating massages, Celebrating You is the luxury day spa without walls.

Lisa Barnes

 Q&A

What are your most popular products or services?
Our fabulous spa parties! Our spa services can be customized to suit the theme of any special event or occasion.

Who is your role model or mentor?
My mother is my role model. As she says, "The race is not given to the swift, nor to the strong, but he who endures." I'm thankful to have her love and support.

What business mistake have you made that you will not repeat?
I will not take shortcuts in marketing. My company provides luxury on-site spa services in the comfort of your home or surroundings. We do not have a retail location, so our website has to speak volumes and show you that Celebrating You has the best spa services.

Sondra Lewis

Q&A

What are your most popular products or services?
Makeup artistry and fashion styling.

People may be surprised to know...
I'm a makeup artist, and I own more than 300 lipsticks! I'm also a fashion stylist, and the fashion and beauty correspondent for an online talk show.

How do you spend your free time?
Going on road trips with family and shopping with my mom and sister. Trying new makeup looks on my friends. Eating at a nice restaurant by myself with a great fashion magazine lets me relax and fuels my creativity.

What is your indulgence?
Lipsticks, cupcakes, chunky jewelry, and handbags are my absolute weaknesses.

Main photo by Paul Butterfield Photography; bottom left photo (opposite page) by Leigh Smyth of Oh Snap! photography; portrait, bottom middle and right photos (opposite page) by RL Campbell Photography

CHIC CHOCOLATE

1.888.792.3597
chicchocolate.net, Twitter: @chicchocolate

Stylish. Fresh. On-trend.
From deep rich chocolate to vanilla chocolate and every flavor
of chocolate in between, Chic Chocolate is a fashionable
lifestyle blog on the "Chocolate City" that is DC!

CHIC PHYSIQUE

4931 St. Elmo Ave, Bethesda, 301.718.2452
chicphysiquefitness.com, Twitter: @chicphysique

Empowering. Confident. Fit.
Chic Physique is one of the premier women's alternative, exotic, and pole dancing fitness studios in the Maryland/northern Virginia/Washington, DC, metro area offering traditional and specialty classes, all within a small studio setting. The main focus of Chic Physique is pole dance fitness classes incorporating dance, acrobatics, strength training and aerobic activity executed through a series of "exercises" on a vertical pole.

Tina
Moran

 Q&A

What are your most popular products or services?
Pole dance fitness, Hula-hoop, and T&A (tush & abs) classes.

People may be surprised to know...
Any person of any age can pole dance!

What or who inspired you to start your business?
The unique way I was getting fit and having fun.

How do you spend your free time?
Spending time with my family and finding new ways to workout.

What is your indulgence?
Mani-pedis and chocolate...

Where is your favorite place to go with your girlfriends?
Any place we can set up the stand-alone pole and jam!

COLOR-CODED
ORGANIZING

866.61.COLOR (866.612.6567)
color-coded.net, Twitter: @ColorCoded

Organized. Efficient. Fun.
Color-Coded Organizing helps busy home and business owners create order
in their most cluttered spaces. Color-Coded Organizing was founded to share
a passion for organization and design. They understand how frustrating
a disorganized space can be. Their mission is to achieve organization in
clients' spaces to increase efficiency, save time, and relieve stress.

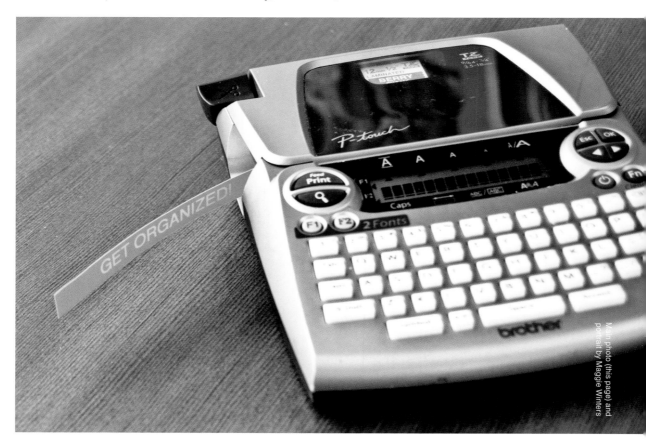

Main photo (this page) and
portrait by Maggie Winters

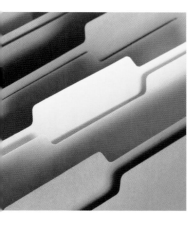
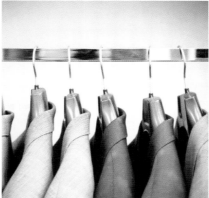

Alejandra Costello

Q&A

People may be surprised to know...
I started my business at the age of 23.

What or who inspired you to start your business?
I believed in myself. When you believe
you can do anything in life, the path
will unravel how you envision it.

Who is your role model or mentor?
I am a big fan of Martha Stewart, except
for the whole insider trading fiasco.

What is your indulgence?
My label maker, bright colors, polka
dots, white chocolate, and poodles.

What do you CRAVE? In business? In life?
I crave freedom, laughter, and turning
challenges into opportunities.

Tazima Ayana Davis

Q&A

What or who inspired you to start your business?
Job frustration, lots of tears, and the possibility that I could enjoy life, assist others, and prosper.

Who is your role model or mentor?
LiYana Silver, relationship expert and coach.

What is your indulgence?
Oats and dark chocolate! It's an official three-way tie between the Salty Oats Cookies at Teaism, Michelle's Cherry Chocolate Almond Granola, and Dagoba's Lavender Blueberry Dark Chocolate.

Where is your favorite place to go with your girlfriends?
Thrift boutique shopping, better if near a beach, and even better if we can follow it up with yoga.

COMPASSIONATE RENEGADE

202.328.1471
compassionaterenegade.com, Twitter: @Compassion8Rngd

Honest. Loving. Fierce.
Compassionate Renegade was formed to help bold, outwardly accomplished women experience deeper meaning, greater self-expression, and true fulfillment. Compassionate Renegade's life purpose coaching honors each client's particular interests and talents in order to cultivate a lifestyle that delivers satisfaction, sustainable prosperity, and joy.

CORE CONNECTION LIFESTYLE

866.611.5546
coreconnectionlifestyle.com, Twitter: @coreconnection

Inviting. Motivational. Limitless.
Core Connection Lifestyle is a wellness-based company dedicated to empowering women with the essential tools to optimize their lives. Through health counseling, lifestyle coaching, and speaking, Takeyah A. Young empowers successful, yet over-stressed professional and entrepreneurial women to reconnect with their core values so they can experience fulfillment, happiness, and balance in all areas of their lives.

Takeyah A. Young

 Q&A

What are your most popular products or services?
My life balance breakthrough sessions give clients clear steps for transforming their lives, and the motivation to actually make it happen.

People may be surprised to know...
I am a trained engineer, so my problem-solving is intuition-led, yet infused with innovative analysis and strategy.

Who is your role model or mentor?
My mother served as my fabulous role model through her hard work, integrity, and quiet sophistication.

How do you spend your free time?
Traveling, crafting, and reading way too many design blogs.

Christie Askew

Q&A

What are your most popular products or services?
Our custom couture gift bags and boxes. They are perfect for any social event, wedding, or that special someone.

People may be surprised to know...
I was Miss Maryland USA 2000 and competed at the nationally televised 2000 Miss USA Pageant.

What or who inspired you to start your business?
After 18 months of planning my own wedding, I knew I wanted to share my attention to detail with others.

Who is your role model or mentor?
My mother. She is a strong, giving, and independent woman who has taught me to believe in myself and never lose sight of my dreams. She is truly my right hand.

COUTURE MEETS CHIC

202.421.7956
couturemeetschic.com

Chic. Couture. Creative

Couture Meets Chic is a full-service wedding and event planning company specializing in the most intimate of social events to elaborate destination and Washington weddings. They also feature one-of-a-kind custom couture gift bags and boxes that are perfect for a weekend at the beach, a chic mom-to-be or that wedding to remember.

WEDDING BOARDING PASS
DAVIS/KEITH
11A
DATE
11 OCTOBER 09
DESTINATION
ST. THOMAS
U.S. VIRGIN ISLANDS

This is your Ticket to Save the Date

CURRENT BOUTIQUE

2529 Wilson Blvd, Arlington, 703.528.3079
1009 King St, Alexandria, 703.549.2272
currentboutique.com, Twitter: @currentboutique

Modern. Bold. Eco-friendly.

Current Boutique offers customers handpicked consignment pieces that fit the criteria of great quality, style, cut, and color. Ladies need a revolving wardrobe: you wear an outfit once or twice, pictures are taken, everyone's seen you in it, and you can't wear it again. Current Boutique is the best place to recycle your wardrobe. Turn your cluttered closet into cash now at this no-appointment-necessary boutique.

Photos by Eddie Paylor

Carmen Lopez

 # Q&A

What are your most popular
products or services?
Most ladies come in looking for fun dresses!
They want a great piece for dates, dinners, and
social events. The hot sellers range from casual
day dresses to sexy numbers that will wow their
man or get compliments from their girlfriends.

People may be surprised to know...
Current Boutique also sells new
handpicked dresses and jewelry from
design houses in NY and LA.

How do you spend your free time?
I love to cook. It's very relaxing for me. My
favorite right now is a whole grain pasta
dish with sausage, broccoli, kale, sun-
dried tomatoes, and tons of garlic!

Nakia Fisher

Q&A

What or who inspired you to start your business?
I remember showcasing my first jewelry designs to close friends and family; they were in awe that I actually made the pieces and wanted to know how much they were. I knew I was onto something from that moment.

People may be surprised to know...
I have a degree in information technology and another in interior design. I love designing logos!

Who is your role model or mentor?
Lisa Price, the creator of Carol's Daughter, is my role model. After reading her book *Success Never Smelled So Sweet*, I absolutely knew my creative ideas would manifest!

What is your indulgence?
Red Velvet cupcakes and coffee ice cream!

CYNIRJE CULTURE BY DESIGN

888.729.6475
cynirje.com, Twitter: @cynirje

Distinctive. Bold. Beautiful.
Cynirje Culture by Design features an eclectic mix of handmade, sophisticated, and bold fashion and home accessories. The statement semi-precious gemstone necklaces are handmade and designed by owner Nakia Fisher as a manifestation of her creative thoughts about the world.

THE DANDELION PATCH

111 Church St NW, Vienna, 703.319.9099
11923 Market St, Reston, 703.689.2240
thedandelionpatch.com

Friendly. Knowledgeable. Fashionable.
The Dandelion Patch is a fine stationery and gift boutique with
locations in Vienna and Reston, Virginia. Since 1994, they've been
specializing in custom invitations for all of life's milestones. They
know their customers by name and their product by heart.

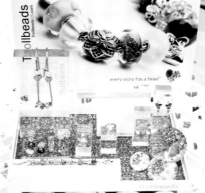

Heidi Kallett

Q&A

What are your most popular products or services?
By far, we are best known for our custom wedding invitation ensembles and our wide selection of personal gifts.

What or who inspired you to start your business?
With my love of entertaining, fondness of tradition, and respect for the latest fashion trends, it's no surprise that I love being a stationery retailer.

Who is your role model or mentor?
I've had many mentors throughout my life, and they have all impacted who I am today. The one common thread is that they've all been optimistic, driven, and smart.

How do you spend your free time?
When I have a moment and the weather cooperates, there is nothing better than a long run with my favorite tunes and no schedule.

DATING COACH
JESS MCCANN

240.AT.HELLO (240.284.3556)
jessmccann.com, Twitter: @ulosthimathello

Enlightening. Game-changing. Results-oriented.
Jess McCann, author of *You Lost Him at Hello*, is a DC-based dating coach and relationship expert who helps men and women take control of their love lives. Jess has appeared on nationally televised shows such as *Good Morning America*, *Extra*, and the *Fox Morning News*, and writes a column for *Washington Life Magazine* called "The Dating Scene."

Jess McCann

People may be surprised to know...
I used to be terrible at dating but
now I am happily married at 33.

What or who inspired you to start your business?
I used to own an outsourced sales
company and was inspired by the uncanny
parallel between sales and dating.

What business mistake have you
made that you will not repeat?
There was a time I thought I had
achieved my goals and I got complacent.
That's when the bottom fell out. I will
never become complacent again.

Where is your favorite place to
go with your girlfriends?
We love going to brunch! We love Perry's,
Peacock, Urbana, Harry's Tap Room... The
city has so many great places to brunch.

Bradley Wellness photographed by
Meredith Rizzo Photography

What do you CRAVE? In business? In life?

"To be the best, to offer the best, and to make women feel and look great—total happiness."

Cathy Campbell of Details of Occoquan

THE WASHINGTON BALLET
WONDERLAND

Pum Lefebure

Q&A

What are your most popular
products or services?
Graphic design: branding, annual
reports, websites, art direction,
and product development.

People may be surprised to know...
Design Army is an internationally
known design firm.

What or who inspired you to start your business?
My mother. She sent me to the US
as a exchange student, and I did not
know a single word of English. Within
a year I knew I could do anything.

What do you CRAVE? In business? In life?
I crave being the best. Second
place is a dirty word.

▶ DESIGN ARMY

510 H St NE, Washington, 202.797.1018
designarmy.com, Twitter: @designarmy

Creative. Smart. Stylish.

Design Army prides itself on being smart, strategic, and selective. They focus on creating meaningful visuals for the public and private sector, nonprofits, artists, and the occasional politician. Working in diverse media including print, interactive, packaging, environmental, and editorial allows them to produce design that is multipurpose. Design that resonates. Design that transforms.

Top left and middle photos (opposite page) by Erik Johnson

Sherry Ways and
Susan Schemm

 Q&A

What are your most popular products or services?
Our most popular services are interior color consultations, window treatment designs, feng shui redesigns, and flooring selections. Most popular products include fabrics and area rugs.

People may be surprised to know...
Twins are the common denominator in both Susan's and Sherry's lives. Susan has twin boys, Sherry is a twin herself, and even Sherry's cat is a twin!

What or who inspired you to start your business?
Our love of interior design inspired us to start this business. We are both passionate about creating beautiful, functional spaces for people to enjoy. Our motto: "Design for life!"

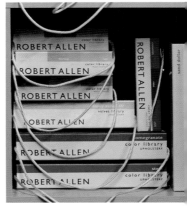

DESIGN SCHEME INTERIORS, LLC

8600 Foundry St, Ste 204, Savage, 301.317.7855
designschemeinteriors.com, Twitter: @designschemeint

Sustainable. Cutting-edge. Zen.
Design Scheme Interiors is a full-service interior decor firm specializing in both residential and commercial interiors. Their services are designed to meet the needs of a large range of projects, from basic decorating to major remodeling. Starting with an initial consultation to help you define your requirements, services include home staging, feng shui, and eco-friendly designs.

DETAILS OF OCCOQUAN

206 Mill St, Occoquan, 703.494.4959
detailsofoccoquan.net

Unique. Experienced. Service-oriented.
Details of Occoquan is a ladies specialty boutique located in historic Occoquan, Virginia. They are known for unparalled customer service, sizing from 2 to 22, and fabulous, unique, and unusual clothing and accessories. They offer custom-fitted bras and shapewear, private consultations, and private shopping nights. The environment is warm and inviting, bringing customers back frequently.

Cathy Campbell

Details
Of Occoquan

Fashion & Accessories
for Today's Fabulous Woman

206 MILL
STREET

Q&A

What are your most popular
products or services?
Lee Andersen art-to-wear clothing,
Joseph Ribkoff, Frank Lyman, Onesole
sandals, Chamilia beads, Wacoal
America, and great customer service.

Who is your role model or mentor?
Ursula LaFond, previous owner who
allowed me to fulfill my dream of buying
and owning a fabulous store.

What do you CRAVE? In business? In life?
To be the best, to offer the best, to make
women feel and look great, total happiness.

What or who inspired you to start your business?
My Aunt Phyllis, who introduced me to
fashion, people I've worked for who always
said no, and going into business for myself.

Cindy McCartney

Q&A

What are your most popular products or services?
Our designer clothing, handbags, and shoes, and our really fabulous line of well-priced fashion jewelry. We tailor the Diva experience to each client, and quite often help them solve "fashion 911" situations, such as, "I have a black-tie affair to go to tonight, and I need a dress..."

Who is your role model or mentor?
My parents. I've learned so much from them about how to treat people. Conversely, all the bad bosses I've ever had, for showing me how never to treat people.

What business mistake have you made that you will not repeat?
Mistakes are okay as long as you learn from them. We added bridal consignment for a while, and it was just not right for us. The takeaway was: always keep your brand's core focus.

DIVA DESIGNER CONSIGNMENT & OTHER DELIGHTS

116 S Pitt St, Alexandria, 703.683.1022
divaboutiqueva.com, Twitter: @DivaBoutiqueVA

Stylish. Vibrant. Fun.
Diva Designer Consignment & Other Delights is a must-shop for fashionistas who love designer clothing and accessories, but don't love designer prices. Shoppers will find items by DVF, PRADA, Milly, Tory Burch, Jimmy Choo, CHANEL, and many other great brands, and the selection changes every day. If you enjoy "the hunt," you'll love Diva!

Photos by Meredith Rizzo Photography

DOLCE STUDIO FILMS

📞

$

703.300.9033
dolcestudiofilms.com, Twitter: @dolcestudiofilm

Fresh. Joyous. Artful.
Dolce Studio Films is an award-winning company that specializes in fresh
event filmmaking. They focus on capturing not just the public performance
aspect of your day, but also the joy, attitude, mood, and impermanent
sweetness of life. Then they take those captured moments in time and
artfully create a permanent motion-picture window to your past.

Haynal Papp

Q&A

People may be surprised to know...
You will hardly know we're filming. Our style is unobtrusive. It won't feel as though a Hollywood crew has descended on your big day. We're like the Secret Service—dressed in black and part of the background!

What business mistake have you made that you will not repeat?
Making a business decision I felt ambivalent about. If your gut tells you, "no," don't give away your power by letting your head convince you otherwise. Running your own business is stressful enough—every decision should be based on research, numbers, and your intuition.

How do you spend your free time?
Reading, writing, walking, shopping, connecting with friends, playing with my girls, visiting family, and, of course, watching movies!

Christine Njoora and
Kechia Taylor

Q&A

What or who inspired you to start your business?
Kechia: My sister has always inspired me to pursue business through her words of wisdom and support. Also, having a love of art, beauty, and fashion has been a constant for me.
Christine: The desire for independence and the satisfaction of working for myself.

Who is your role model or mentor?
Kechia: Damone Roberts of Damone Roberts Beverly Hills is my role model.
Christine: My mother who has started several businesses and been very successful.

What is your indulgence?
Kechia: A perfect set of brows, chandelier earrings, Viva Glam lipstick and, of course, a daily dose of Reese's Peanut Butter Cups and a Coke.
Christine: Shoes and my beauty sleep.

ECOBLISS
SALON AND SPA

1702 Transportation Blvd, Ste H, Crofton, 410.451.8088
ecoblisssalonandspa.com, Twitter: @ecoblisssalon

Green. Modern. Stylish.

EcoBliss is an Aveda Concept salon and spa created by fusing a passion for the beauty industry with a commitment to the environment. Owners Kechia Taylor and Christine Njoora's mission is to prove that we can be beautiful and indulge in our daily beauty regimens without endangering the planet with harmful chemical waste.

Photos by Meredith Rizzo Photography

Cheryle Robison, Christie Bell,
and Katie Mandell

Q&A

People may be surprised to know...
We donate our blankets to ill children worldwide,
and give a portion of all sales to pediatric brain
tumor research and family support programs.

What or who inspired you to start your business?
Our daughters. We began sewing blankets
to give them the best, and started our
business to share them with others.

Who is your role model or mentor?
Katie's daughter, Emily. She showed incredible
courage and strength during her two short years.
Her ability to keep smiling and show others what
love is makes her a role model for all of us.

How do you spend your free time?
Our free time is spent playing with our kids,
husbands, extended family, and dogs!

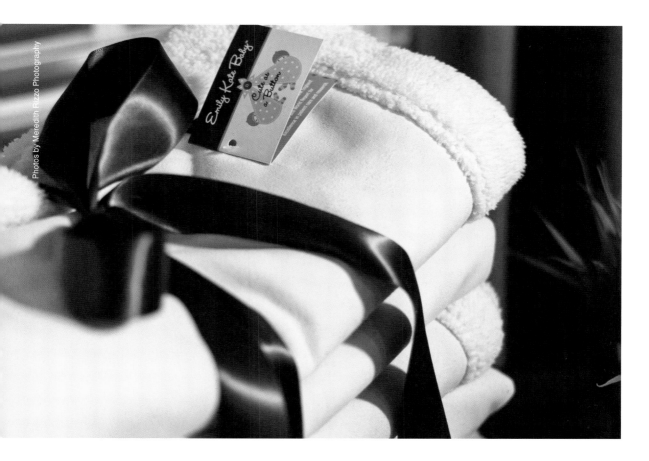

EMILY KATE BABY

$

800.594.4520
emilykatebaby.com

Classic. Cuddly. Chic.
Emily Kate Baby designs and manufactures heirloom-quality baby blankets, bibs, burp cloths, and accessories. Signature products are lovingly handmade in the United States, using premium fabrics. All items come with a guarantee of extraordinary quality and cute-as-a-button classic American style. Browse their extensive online store and find the perfect something for the little one in your life.

ENGAGING AFFAIRS

888.481.5156
engagingaffairs.com, Twitter: @bridalbubbly

Innovative. Chic. Fun.
Engaging Affairs is one of the DC area's top wedding planning companies, creating some of the most fabulous and fun events in the city and beyond. From sophisticated and elegant to vintage and charming, Engaging Affairs weddings are custom-designed for each couple and are recognized for their personalized details, impeccable styling, and seamless planning. Engaging Affairs weddings are more than memorable, they're unforgettable.

Laura Weatherly

Q&A

What are your most popular products or services?
Most brides hire us to plan their weddings from beginning to end. We also offer a sanity-saving "Day-Of" package for brides who need help pulling it all together at the end.

People may be surprised to know...
We can save brides a lot of money. And we don't wear headphones on the wedding day like J. Lo did in The Wedding Planner. We get asked that a lot!

What is your indulgence?
My after-wedding indulgence is a super-sized Coke Slurpee and my after wedding season treat is a day at The Mandarin Spa.

Where is your favorite place to go with your girlfriends?
In DC, Baked & Wired for a serious sugar rush. Outside DC, Rancho La Puerta for serious rejuvenation.

ENJOI CUPCAKES

202.642.2281
enjoicupcakes.com, Twitter: @EnjoiCupcakes

Delectable. Innovative. Trendsetting.
EnJoi Cupcakes is a premier mobile/delivery cupcake service. Cupcakes are made to order and then available to be delivered to your home, event, office, etc. Using only the finest ingredients from local grocers and nondairy products such as almond milk, their recipes are sure to take you back to your days as a child when everything was full of love and goodness.

Photos by Larry Wade Photography

Carla Carter

Q&A

What are your most popular
products or services?
Sweet Potato Cupcake, Oma's Lemony Lemon,
Baileys® Irish Cream, and Classic Red Velvet.

Who is your role model or mentor?
My mother is the matriarch of our family.
Truly an awesome woman with strong
beliefs and superb baking skills.

What is your indulgence?
Any opportunity to use my passport,
spa treatments, and, of course,
shopping for boots and bags.

Where is your favorite place to
go with your girlfriends?
The @ttic, one of DC's best poetry spots.

Adrien Cotton

Q&A

People may be surprised to know...
We have 18 classes, each tailored to our individual clients. Our personal fitness trainers all had a background outside of fitness before they worked in fitness. We range from corporate executives and policy wonks, to financial analysts.

What or who inspired you to start your business?
After a challenging 16-year career in politics and public policy, I didn't believe I was helping anyone. In this business, I help people daily. Young or old, thin or overweight, male or female, people who are unaware of the simple changes they can make to live a healthier lifestyle. Helping clients reach, and even exceed, their fitness and wellness goals is incredibly gratifying.

FITNESS ON THE RUN

109 S Alfred St, Alexandria, 703.299.9333
fitnessontherun.net

Efficient. Personal. All-encompassing.
Fitness on the Run is Old Town Alexandria's premier fitness studio,
offering private personal training, including strength training, kettlebells,
CrossFit, and a wide range of group fitness classes. They provide the
right activities to help clients meet and maintain their individual wellness
goals. Group classes are appropriate for all ages and fitness levels,
and provide every client with the ultimate personal attention.

FORNASH

3222 M St NW, Ste W-229, Washington, 202.338.0774
fornash.com

Fabulous. Classic. Affordable.

Through its Georgetown boutique and wholesale business, Fornash offers unique accessories, personalized gifts, and original designs. With a mission to make fabulous fashion accessible to everyone, owner Stephanie Fornash Kennedy designs with a classic, contemporary approach and seeks out unique, affordable products. Fornash sells to more than 1,000 retail stores worldwide.

Stephanie Fornash Kennedy

Q&A

What are your most popular products or services?
The Boa Scarf (which was featured on Oprah's "O List" in the December 2009 issue), starfish earrings, and affordable fashionable enamel jewelry.

What or who inspired you to start your business?
I needed an outlet for my creativity and passion for fashion. I turned a hobby into a successful career after I was laid off from my 9-to-5 consulting job. I am a true believer that when one door closes another one opens!

Where is your favorite place to go with your girlfriends?
Barrel Oak Winery in Delaplane, Virginia. A trip out to the country is always good for the soul... and the Virginia wine isn't bad either!

Georgetown

Ann Snow and
Michelle Snow Bracken

Q&A

What are your most popular
products or services?
Our cupcakes are the showpiece of our
bakeshop, but it's the other delicacies
that make coming to Frosting a true,
all-around, joyous experience.

People may be surprised to know...
We serve coffee and espresso in the
traditional Italian way. Our cupcakes
and coffee are the perfect marriage!

What is your indulgence?
When you work the hours we do, getting
off our feet is a true indulgence... and
we completely savor every moment!

What business mistake have you
made that you will not repeat?
Hiring friends/acquaintances. No
business is worth losing a friend over.

FROSTING BAKESHOP & COFFEE BAR

1 Wisconsin Circle, Chevy Chase, 301.539.9021
frostingacupcakery.com, Twitter: @frostingdc

Simple. Sweet. Happy.
Frosting is a boutique bakeshop and coffee bar in the heart of the Chevy Chase shopping district. Their specialty is *small. round. joy.* sweets (cupcakes), but they also offer all of the comfort treats your mother used to make and a full coffee and espresso bar by illy to boot!

Photos by Kate Headley

Chevy Chase

THE FULL CUP

218 N Lee St, Ste 206, Alexandria, 703.836.9441
thefullcup.com, Twitter: @fullcup

Educational. Inspired. Service-oriented.
The Full Cup is a European-inspired bra-fitting salon dedicated to educating
women on the benefits of wearing proper-fitting bras, and, most importantly,
teaching women how to take care of their breasts. The boutique refers
to this holistic approach as "total breast wellness." Certified bra-fitting
experts provide one-on-one attention in a private and relaxed setting.

Photos by Meredith Rizzo Photography, except portrait by Susan Rook

Frances Crespo

Q&A

What are your most popular
products or services?
Our most popular service is educating
women on how a bra should fit. Our most
popular products are comfortable, beautiful
bras and panties from European lines such
as Anita, Aubade, Conturelle, Fantasie,
Freya, Panache, and Prima Donna.

Where is your favorite place to
go with your girlfriends?
Contrary to popular belief, I am a homebody. I
prefer to have a nice meal at home and invite
those closest to me to join in the celebration.

People may be surprised to know...
I am a naval officer and I am honored to serve
my country. At night, I crunch business data
and love using my creative and entrepreneurial
mind to own and grow my business. I also help
other women start and grow their businesses
through Ladies Who Launch–Metro DC.

Photos by Ezra Gregg

GLAMOURHOLICS!

202.465.2576
glamourholics.com, Twitter: @glamourholics

Glamorous. Chic. Stylish.
GlamourHolics! is a shopping soirée uniting chic shopaholics with some of
the area's most unique independent retailers. GlamourHolics! events are held
every spring, summer, fall, and winter/holiday in exciting and entertaining
venues. Hundreds of affluent, hard-working fashionistas look forward to
the five-hour affairs that consist of spectacular shopping, the coveted Glam
Swag Bag, pampering, beauty demos, and glamorous prize giveaways.

Myss R. Stephens

Q&A

What are your most popular products or services?
Our Glam Swag Bags are a big deal for early-arriving guests. They absolutely adore the treats and trinkets!

What or who inspired you to start your business?
The need for a more consistent platform where independant designers without a brick-and-mortar store could sell and showcase their merchandise.

What is your indulgence?
Vacationing and spending quality time with my husband, our three beautiful daughters, and my close friends!

Where is your favorite place to go with your girlfriends?
Having a slumber party! We love lounging around, eating, and sipping our favorite drinks, all while sharing our accomplishments, dreams, and fears.

What is your indulgence?

" *Spending endless hours on late August afternoons scouring the September issue of* Vogue. "

Julia Farr of Julia Farr

GREEN-À-PORTER

301.379.9352
greeenaporter.com, Twitter: @greenaporter

Glamorous. Conscientious. Green.
Green-à-Porter was inspired by owners Adriana Seligman and Amy Katz's desire to make a difference. By enlisting their favorite boutiques, they created a program to help the shopping community participate in the world's efforts to go green. At a time when waste is anything but glamorous, the Green-à-Porter program provides retailers and consumers the opportunity to help the world while they shop.

Amy Katz and Adriana Seligman

Q&A

People may be surprised to know...
According to The Wall Street Journal, the
United States goes through 100 billion
plastic shopping bags annually. By joining
forces, we can dramatically reduce the
damage we do to our environment.

What or who inspired you to start your business?
Through years of friendship, long playdates and
hours at Starbucks, we inspired each other to
take a risk on an idea that we truly believe in.

Where is your favorite place to
go with your girlfriends?
Shopping in Georgetown, coffee at Leopold's,
yogurt at Sweet Green's, and dinner at Raku.

What do you CRAVE? In business? In life?
Balance. Being a good business
partner, wife, friend, mother, and, most
importantly, being true to ourselves.

Penny Karas

Q&A

What are your most popular products or services?
Our daily selection of 16 to 18 cupcake flavors; special custom-decorated, seasonal or themed cupcakes; and cupcake decorating classes.

What or who inspired you to start your business?
I wanted to turn my passion for gourmet baked goodies into more than a hobby— something I could do as a vocation and bring smiles to people's faces everyday.

What do you CRAVE? In business? In life?
What I crave in business and in life are the same: uplifting, fulfilling relationships, constant learning and growing, putting smiles on peoples' faces, day-to-day joy, and long-term contentment.

HELLO CUPCAKE

1361 Connecticut Ave NW, Washington, 202.861.2253
hellocupcakeonline.com

Delicious. Beautiful. Creative.
At Hello Cupcake in Dupont Circle, gourmet cupcakes are made fresh from
scratch, all day, every day. Using the highest quality all-natural seasonal and
local ingredients, they create distinctive treats, each a delightful little gem. With
more than 50 flavors, including vegan and gluten-free varieties, it is easy to find
a favorite. Hello Cupcake is a sophisticated twist on an old-fashioned classic!

Photos by Patrick Onofre Photography

HOLECO® LIFE

301.540.0879
holecolife.com, Twitter: @holecolife

Non-toxic. Organic. Vegan.
Holeco® life is dedicated to the belief that true beauty begins within and extends
to the outside world. Their eco-conscious personal care, mineral cosmetic
makeup and superfoods are handmade with love using the highest quality of
natural ingredients, pure organic extracts, and therapeutic-grade essential
oils, all without the use of synthetic preservatives. A portion of all holeco® life
proceeds goes to International Lifeline Fund projects, which help improve the
quality of life for women and children in developing countries of Africa.

Honi Borden

Q&A

People may be surprised to know...
Most of our special effect pigments contained in our loose powder cosmetics are ECOCERT certified. Some of our products have multiple uses, such as brush cleaner spray that can also be used as air freshener.

What or who inspired you to start your business?
After learning about my son's endocrine imbalance and my husband's and other son's skin allergies, extensive research led me to make a correlation between the use of personal care products containing synthetic preservatives and our well-being. I was inspired to produce the safest lifestyle products for everyone to use with kindness to environment in mind.

How do you spend your free time?
Daily meditation, yoga, mindful reading, playing with my children, and connecting with individuals who desire to be a positive force for higher consciousness are ways in which I mindfully spend my free time.

Jenn Schwartz

Q&A

People may be surprised to know...
How much their lives can be influenced
by intentional, controlled exercise.

What or who inspired you to start your business?
The rising number of preventable injuries and
the irrefutable need for strength enhancement
in female athletes and my clients.

Where is your favorite place to
go with your girlfriends?
In the middle of a humid DC August, we go to
Maine for some hiking, lobster, and white wine!

What do you CRAVE? In business? In life?
Making an impact on women so that
they can intentionally create healthy,
happy lives for themselves.

IMPACT FITNESS DC

571.432.8430
impactfitnessdc.com, Twitter: @ImpactFitnessDC

Effective. Energetic. Influential.
Impact Fitness DC is a dynamic fitness training company specializing in women's fitness needs. They focus both on the female athlete and those serious about making a positive impact on their overall wellness. They are proud to serve as an advocate for young female athletes, and they teach women of all ages how to incorporate exercise to achieve goals and overcome physical barriers.

INDULGE MOBILE SPA

800.289.5850
ndulgemobilespa.com, Twitter: @indulgeecospa

ECO-CHIC BODY CARE

ecochicbodycare.com

Fun. Relaxing. Green.

Indulge Mobile Spa is a luxurious, sustainable company providing clients with top-notch spa services at their home, office, or special event. Transforming each space into a wonderful oasis of tranquility, Indulge Mobile Spa offers therapeutic massage therapy, manicures and pedicures, and salon-quality facials. You bring the guests; they'll bring the rest!

Tammy Carmon

Q&A

What are your most popular products or services?
The lavender spa package, which includes a 30-minute massage and spa pedicure.

Who is your role model or mentor?
Kimora Lee Simmons and Donald Trump.

What business mistake have you made that you will not repeat?
Overspending on advertising and buying too much inventory. Simple is better!

What is your indulgence?
I really do not have any indulgences. I live a really simple life.

What do you CRAVE? In business? In life?
Peace, love, prosperity, good health, and happiness.

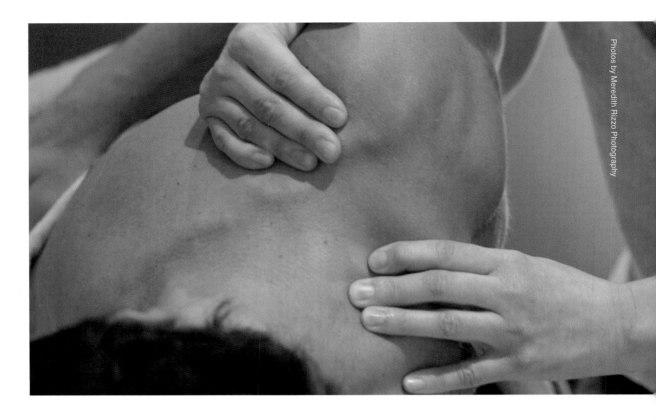

INSPIRE YOUR BODY MASSAGE

4609 Willow Lane, Chevy Chase, 240.381.4898
inspireyourbodymt.com

Fresh. Energizing. Intuitive.

Inspire Your Body Massage is a premier massage service specifically geared toward sports and chronic pain management. Not for the faint of heart, their massage is deep and transforming. Whether you're training for a race or have been living with an old injury or ache, this is the place to come for restorative results.

Naomi Gonzalez

 **Q&A**

What or who inspired you to start your business?
At 5 years old, I remember dreaming I would massage Olympic athletes in Greece. 25 years later, that dream came true. My business is a direct extension of that dream.

People may be surprised to know...
The tattoo on my back is also my business logo, symbolizing the release of old habits that no longer serve us.

How do you spend your free time?
Wine tasting and visiting art galleries.

Where is your favorite place to go with your girlfriends?
Addie's in Rockville. Delicious, organic, and they support local farmers.

What do you CRAVE? In business? In life?
Success and happiness.

Chevy Chase

Rochel Roland

Q&A

What are your most popular
products or services?
Our signature bath salts and handmade
botanical soaps—Citrus Buzz, Ginger
Snap, Green Tea Glee, Mellow Yellow,
'Nilla Buttermilk, and Oatsy Floatsie.

How do you spend your free time?
I am a competitive short-track speedskater,
so I work out and take a lot of baths.

What is your indulgence?
Coffee and chocolate and, of
course, a nice, hot soak.

What do you CRAVE? In business? In life?
I love making people feel good,
and I'm delighted that I can do
that through Joyful Bath Co.

JOYFUL BATH CO.

4948 St. Elmo Ave, Ste 201, Bethesda, 301.986.5320
joyfulbathco.com, Twitter: @joyfulbathco

Relaxing. Refreshing. Reinvigorating.
Joyful Bath Co.'s signature bath salts and handmade botanical soaps blend
the healing elements of the land and the sea with bathing rituals and remedies
from around the world. Natural ingredients include mineral-rich salts from the
Mediterranean and Dead Seas; organic extra virgin olive, palm and coconut oils
mix with honey, buttermilk, ginger root, green tea, oats, coconut milk and pure
essential oils. Create the ultimate bathing experience with Joyful Bath Co.

Photos by Meredith Rizzo Photography

Julia Farr

Q&A

What are your most popular products or services?
Our signature services include the custom-made Julia Farr essential "it" pieces, the holistic Wardrobe Review and Renewal, and accessory trunk shows celebrating DC's female designers.

Who is your role model or mentor?
Kara Ross is an excellent friend and mentor. She is a gifted accessories designer and owner of Kara Ross New York. She's been incredibly generous with her time and creative ideas.

What is your indulgence?
Spending endless hours on late August afternoons scouring the September issue of *Vogue*.

JULIA FARR

5232 44th St NW, Washington, 202.364.FARR (3277)
juliafarrdc.com

Essential. Elegant. Enlightened.
Located in the shopping district of Friendship Heights, the showroom boutique of Julia Farr features wardrobe essentials from both established and emerging designers. Its Zen-like setting with comfortable couches, jazz music, and sparkling refreshments creates a blissful shopping experience. But why stop there? Sit down with Julia to design your own custom-made pieces that blend seamlessly with your existing wardrobe.

KARIN'S FLORIST

527 Maple Ave E, Vienna, 703.281.4141
karinsflorist.com, Twitter: @karinsflorist

Unique. Exquisite. Service-oriented.

Karin's Florist has been family-owned and operated since 1956. They offer creative floral arrangements, custom gift baskets, wines and Champagnes, plants, and more. In addition, their international design team can design your perfect wedding or event, with delivery around the corner or across the world. Since customer service and quality are their first priority, they will make your vision become a reality.

Maris Angolia

 # Q&A

What are your most popular products or services?
Floral arrangements, gourmet baskets, chocolates, wines and champagnes.

What or who inspired you to start your business?
My father and grandfather started the business in 1956. It is an honor to continue their legacy.

What business mistake have you made that you will not repeat?
Putting great employees in the wrong position.

Where is your favorite place to go with your girlfriends?
To the spa to get pampered after a long week!

What do you CRAVE? In business? In life?
In business, to always be on the cutting edge of creative designs, technology, and marketing. In life, to be able to make a positive difference in the lives of the people around me.

Vienna

Nancy Purves Pollard

 Q&A

What are your most popular products or services?
Mauviel cookware, chocolate couverture, knife sharpening, baking supplies, and kitchen equipment.

People may be surprised to know...
We have real Neopolitan pizza flour, and our green cleaning and laundry supplies are first-rate.

How do you spend your free time?
Cooking, reading, container gardening, practicing Pilates, and playing racquetball.

What do you CRAVE? In business? In life?
In business, to be profitable and have fun. In life, a vacation house in Italy.

LA CUISINE
THE COOK'S RESOURCE

323 Cameron St, Alexandria, 1.800.521.1176
lacuisineus.com, Twitter: @cuisinette

Top-notch. Humorous. Green.
Since 1970, La Cuisine has been a destination store for both home and professional cooks. Through their website, they provide great cookware, hard-to-find ingredients, and useful kitchen tools and supplies no matter where you are. They do have some fun stuff for entertaining, too.

LAURA LEE DESIGNS

703.850.3114
lauraleedesigns.com, Twitter: @lauraleedesigns

Unique. Exclusive. Eclectic.
Laura Lee Designs (LLD) creates and manufactures exquisite, high-quality beaded handbags. Hand-crafted with unique combinations of beads, snakeskin, leather, and globally inspired fabrics, these one-of-a-kind creations can have upwards of 25,000 hand-sewn beads and can be used for every occasion. By applying 3D beadwork with vibrant colors and classic design, LLD defines individuality!

Photos by Patrick Onofre Photography

Laura Lee Williams

Q & A

What or who inspired you to start your business?
I listened to my heart as to the right time to step out of the corporate world and transition into what is now Laura Lee Designs.

Who is your role model or mentor?
My mom, my grandmother, and my auntie, all strong women who teach by example.

What business mistake have you made that you will not repeat?
Hiring a PR firm without researching whether or not they have represented who they say they represent!

What is your indulgence?
Theater popcorn. I get the largest size possible!

Where is your favorite place to go with your girlfriends?
Any of our favorite restaurants with great wine, jazz, and positive attitudes!

Angela Phelps

Q&A

People may be surprised to know...
We merchandise new products with
vintage items like typewriters, desks,
and cameras from the early 1900s.

What or who inspired you to start your business?
The need for more retail shops in Shirlington,
and a love for unique and stylish paper goods.

Who is your role model or mentor?
Entrepreneur, author, Food Network chef, and
overall Queen of Fabulocity, Ina Garten.

Where is your favorite place to
go with your girlfriends?
The Carlyle Grand in Shirlington.

What do you CRAVE? In business? In life?
Above all, balance in every aspect of my life.
When my life is in balance, I'm at my best.

LE VILLAGE MARCHE

4150 Campbell Ave, Ste 101, Arlington, 703.379.4444
levillagemarche.com, Twitter: @levillagemarche

VERBENA PAPER & GIFTS

2800 S Randolph St, Ste 110-A, Arlington, 703.379.7001
verbenapaper.com, Twitter: @verbenapaper

Unique. Vibrant. Green.
From letterpress cards and boxed notes to leather journals, linen photo albums
and everything for the chic home office, Verbena Paper & Gifts is a retreat
for those who love all things paper. Located in the Village at Shirlington in
Arlington, Verbena debuted in October 2009. It is the second venture for owner
Angela Phelps, who opened Parisian-inspired Le Village Marche in 2007.

Photos by Patrick Onofre Photography

Lori Graham

Q&A

What are your most popular products or services?
Clients love combining our artistic services, such as concept development and space planning, with our technical services of specification and procurement of art, custom furnishings, and unique accessories. Our best selling product from my custom line, LG Place, is our Camus Sofa which is on our website.

What or who inspired you to start your business?
Three personal renovations that resulted in continued requests to help friends and colleagues on their respective projects.

Who is your role model or mentor?
I fancy myself geographically and aesthetically grounded between England's Kelly Hoppen and Los Angeles' Kelly Wearstler.

LORI GRAHAM DESIGN

1604 17th St NW, Washington, 202.745.0118
lorigraham.com

Chic. Comfortable. Classic.
A design firm with clients nationwide, Lori Graham Design combines Old
World charm with urban flair, using fresh colors, layers of texture, and
modern materials. Lori has been lauded for her ability to marry contemporary
materials with architectural, historical, and environmental elements that
create personalized spaces and transform houses into unique homes.

Photos by Erik Johnson, except portrait by Tyler Mallory

MASH PIT

202.596.8918
mash-pit.org, Twitter: @mashpitorg

Calming. Understanding. Healing.
Somewhere between having a good time at a show and a too-late 911 call, there is MASH PIT: a nonjudgmental, roving critical-care medical crew that promotes the health and well-being of event patrons and artists by providing accessible, low-stress, high-quality medical care on-site at festivals and shows. MASH PIT is a charitable organization.

Analena Valdes Graham

People may be surprised to know...
Apart from being one of the founders and CEO of MASH PIT, I work full time as a medevac nurse for a local trauma center. In addition to healing and music, I love to make people look amazing with my custom-designed corsets that enhance one's natural beauty and promote self-confidence.

What or who inspired you to start your business?
My brother who is in the music business inspired me to start MASH PIT. This was completely artist-driven: "Keep them safe, healthy, and make it a positive experience." I knew there was a need for a handpicked group of competent medical professionals on-site, actively roaming and interacting with the crowd.

What do you CRAVE? In business? In life?
I crave being healthy and doing some good in this world. I will always keep my head up high and make things happen because I don't just dream about it. I live it.

SAYA Originals photographed by Gunnar Larson

What business mistake have you made that you will not repeat?

"*Letting fear get in the way of my bigger vision. I've learned if I can dream it, I certainly can achieve it.*"

Nicole M. Indelicato of Nicole Indelicato

METAMORPHOSIS
WARDROBE &
ACCESSORIES BOUTIQUE

811 Wayne Ave, Silver Spring, 301.588.8901
metamorphosisboutiques.com

Unique. Fabulous. Unforgettable.
One of Silver Spring's best kept secrets, Metamorphosis offers unique high-end fashions at affordable prices. They assist you in expanding your existing wardrobe by accessorizing and introducing new, exciting pieces to coordinate into several outfits. They help you find your best colors and most flattering styles. You will walk away transformed into a wonderful new you!

Photos by Patrick Onofre Photography

Sharon J. Bullock

Q&A

What are your most popular products or services?
Extraordinary hats, handmade costume jewelry, and unique hard-to-find clothing and accessories.

People may be surprised to know...
We offer wardrobe consultations, personal shopping services, color analysis, and cosmetic makeovers.

What or who inspired you to start your business?
Entreprenuership runs in my blood, and I was inspired mostly by my aunt, Faye Burruss, a salon and beauty school owner.

What is your indulgence?
Chocolate, daydreaming about clothes, shopping sprees, entertaining, and decorating my home.

Pixie Windsor

Q&A

What or who inspired you to start your business?
A great love of furniture and decorating. Even when I was a little girl, I was constantly rearranging furniture and painting anything that stood still for too long.

Who is your role model or mentor?
My great aunt left us three houses full of family heirlooms, all procured at auctions. She was a little bit country, a little bit Dorothy Draper!

What business mistake have you made that you will not repeat?
Having more than one location at a time. I've tried it three times and it doesn't work for me. Nor does having a partner; it's gotta be my show.

Where is your favorite place to go with your girlfriends?
Any place out in the elements!

MISS PIXIE'S
FURNISHINGS & WHATNOT...

1626 14th St NW, Washington, 202.232.8171
misspixies.com

Fun. Functional. Affordable.

Miss Pixie's has been selling and delivering vintage home furnishings
and whatnot in the DC area for more than 14 years. Their one-of-a-kind
collections are presented every Thursday, all procured from area auctions.
Everything is priced to move, and by the end of each week, most of the
inventory is gone... so remember, she who hesitates is lost at Miss Pixie's.

Logan Circle

MY BODY MY WAY

1525 Pointer Ridge Pl, Ste 200, Bowie, 301.249.1814
mybodymyway.com, Twitter: @kristinelouis

Fresh. Innovative. Inviting.
The foremost goal at My Body My Way is to have you looking and feeling
your very best. Set in a private, spa-like environment, they offer a variety
of services from personal training and boot camps to yoga and fitness
coaching by phone. Whether utilizing in-studio or long-distance services,
My Body My Way is a great solution to losing weight and staying fit.

Kristine E. Louis

Q&A

What are your most popular
products or services?
Boot Camp and our Body After Baby
Yes Exercise and Fitness Journal
(bodyafterbabyyes.com).

People may be surprised to know...
I don't work out seven days a week.

Who is your role model or mentor?
I am inspired by Angela Bassett for her
awesome physique and commitment to
health. She makes the fifties look great!

What business mistake have you
made that you will not repeat?
Trying to accommodate everyone.
There are riches in niches.

How do you spend your free time?
I am a geek at heart and love spending time
working on our websites and being with my
husband, Dimitri, and sons, Matthew and Elijah.

Cinnamon Bowser

Q&A

What are your most popular
products or services?
Classic warm lotion pedicures, hands down!

What or who inspired you to start your business?
A pregnant girlfriend—she needed
a pedi before she delivered.

Who is your role model or mentor?
My mother is polished, chic, and classic,
as well as smart, wise, loving, and fun.

Where is your favorite place to
go with your girlfriends?
We like to shop, eat, and people-watch,
so Georgetown, National Harbor,
and Old Town are favorites.

NAIL TAXI

703.345.1000
nailtaxi.com, Twitter: @nailtaxi

Polished. Chic. Classic.
Nail Taxi is a premier mobile nail boutique. They send fabulous professional nail technicians out for weddings, corporate events, hospital visits, team building, or whatever you need. Visit Nail Taxi today, and get polished!

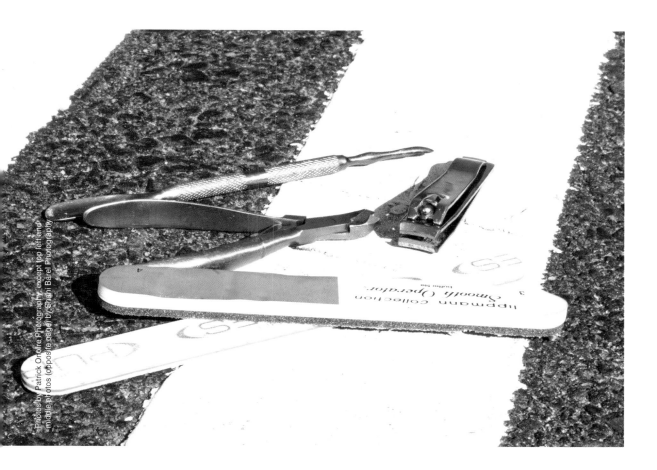

THE NEST EGG

11940 Grand Commons Ave, Fairfax, 703.988.0944
shopthenestegg.com, Twitter: @thenestegg

Unique. Inspiring. Welcoming.
The Nest Egg is one of the area's top local destinations for unique home furnishings, decorative accents, and gifts. The store feathers its nest with inspired pieces ranging from custom-designed, domestic, and imported case goods to upholstered furniture, art, florals, rugs, lighting, and decorative accessories. Gift options include tabletop pieces, candles, soaps, and a very popular selection of baby items.

Photos by Patrick Onofre Photography

Ann O'Shields

Q&A

People may be surprised to know...
You can have beautiful custom furniture that is made in the US and delivered in 4–12 weeks.

What or who inspired you to start your business?
Years ago I discovered a store in the Outer Banks called Urban Cottage. I loved it and longed for more unique local stores in our area.

What is your indulgence?
Soy lattes, good wine, and shopping!

Where is your favorite place to go with your girlfriends?
We like to get together in New York City or at the beach, but we are just as happy meeting locally for dinner or drinks when we can.

What do you CRAVE? In business? In life?
The ability to be present, having things run smoothly, and finding the time to enjoy life!

Jackie Thompson

Q&A

What are your most popular products or services?
Our best-selling artists are Anthony Armstrong, John Holyfield, William Tolliver, Paul Goodnight, Charly Palmer, and Calvin Coleman.

What or who inspired you to start your business?
My passion for art and the desire to leave a legacy for my children.

Who is your role model or mentor?
My parents are my role models. My mother's strength and commitment to family and my father, who, in his 80s, still runs his own business.

What do you CRAVE? In business? In life?
In business, I crave being the first name people think of when they think of quality African American art. In life, I crave the freedom and independence to create beauty, joy, and wealth.

 # OVERDUE RECOGNITION ART GALLERY

6828 B Racetrack Road, Bowie, 301.262.3553
overduerecognition.com

Fine. Impressive. Cultured.
Overdue Recognition Art Gallery proudly represents over 75 renowned
and emerging African American artists. Specializing in everything from
originals to fine art reproductions, including serigraphs, giclées, and limited
and open edition lithographs, they are committed to art as an essential
part of life and therefore exhibit, collect, preserve, and encourage art!

THE PEARL

8171 Maple Lawn Blvd, Ste 100, Fulton, 301.776.6948
thepearlspa.com

Luxurious. Special. Extraordinary.
Located in the prestigious business district of Maple Lawn, Maryland,
this 11,000 square-foot spa features 13 treatment rooms (including two
opulent private suites), an exclusive VIP room with a waterfall shower,
and the signature Blue Grotto, guaranteed to leave you pleading for
more. THE pearl makes extraordinary things happen every day!

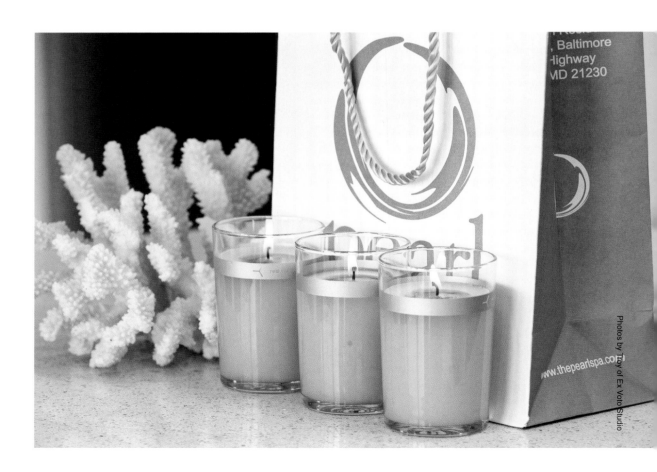

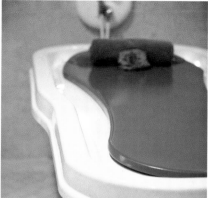

Kassi Buscher

Q&A

What are your most popular products or services?
Icelandic Fusion massage, freshwater pearl facial, and pearltini manicure.

What business mistake have you made that you will not repeat?
Attempting partnerships with people who just did not "get" what we were trying to do. We only do business with partners who share the same values.

What do you CRAVE? In business? In life?
In business, taking care of my special team of pearls. I want them to always believe that with a little hard work and a big dream, anything is possible! In life, to know that I gave 101 percent every day. I am blessed to be on this earth.

What is your indulgence?
I am a bath junkie! I love a hot bath and a good book!

Susan Battle

Q&A

What are your most popular products or services?
Our hand-painted needlepoint canvases and finishing services, from pillows and ornaments to shoes and purses. We also have ghost stitchers who will stitch any project for you.

People may be surprised to know...
Needlepoint is much more than old-fashioned pillows. I stitch purses, shoes, bracelets, and hip Christmas stockings. The world of needlepoint has really opened up.

Who is your role model or mentor?
My grandmother owned a thriving antique shop for years. She loved owning her own business. I wanted to have that same experience of really enjoying my livelihood... and I do!

THE POINT OF IT ALL

5232 44th St NW, Washington, 202.966.9898
tpoia.com

Vibrant. Colorful. Creative.
The Point of it All is a premier needlepoint shop in Washington. They specialize in exciting hand-painted canvases, a diverse array of fibers, and expert finishing, all in a creative, enthusiastic environment.

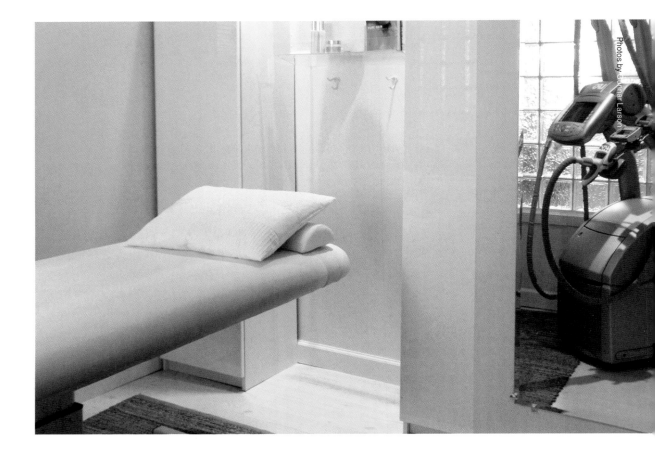

PURESKIN

4609 Willow Lane, Chevy Chase, 301.907.6662
pureskinbethesda.com

Rejuvenating. Pure. Innovative.
Pureskin is a unique micro spa in Chevy Chase, Maryland, where innovative
rejuvenation treatments combine state-of-the-art technology with
luxury beauty products. Non-invasive, holistic, and pampering, each
offering focuses on achieving your most radiant skin. The healthy
beauty of the face and body is the beauty of Pureskin.

Amy Boyce

Q&A

What or who inspired you to start your business?
My wonderful colleague, Karyn Seymour,
has encouraged me from the first suggestion
of Pureskin. Her savvy and discipline make
entrepreneurship look easy, and she unfailingly
finds humor when it is hardest to see!

People may be surprised to know...
Secretly, I wanted to sing country music.

**What business mistake have you
made that you will not repeat?**
The public image of my business did not initially
reflect the warmth and unique feel of Pureskin.

**Where is your favorite place to
go with your girlfriends?**
The Running R Ranch in Bandera, Texas.
What could be better than getting away
on horses in the Texas Hill Country?

Chevy Chase

QUEEN BEE DESIGNS

703.329.6768
queenbeedesigns.com, Twitter: @queenbeebuzz

Stunning. Bold. Affordable.

Founded eight years ago by Allison Priebe Brooks, Queen Bee Designs is one of the premier jewelry design firms in Washington DC. Their pieces are bold, beautiful, and very affordable. When you wear a piece of their jewelry, you are sure to create quite the buzz! Celebs, politicos, socialites, and fashion-savvy women everywhere love Queen Bee!

Photos by Kendra Lewis

Allison Priebe Brooks

Q&A

What are your most popular
products or services?
People love our statement necklaces. Queen
Bee is also known for our gorgeous and
well-priced earrings, rings, and bracelets.

How do you spend your free time?
With my family—my daughter, McClain,
and husband, Michael—they are the
lights of my life. I also write a society and
lifestyle column called BUZZWORTHY for
LocalKicks.com which I really enjoy.

What do you CRAVE? In business? In life?
I love to see effort and people who have an
exuberance for life. I am drawn to people
who are passionate about life and what
they do; not just for a living but how they
live their lives. I always say, "Go big, go
bold, or go home"—that's Queen Bee!

Rita Maximilian and Nicole Foley

Q&A

What are your most popular products or services?
Classes that challenge the body, still the mind, and free the spirit.

People may be surprised to know...
The beautiful studio space looked exactly like that when I found it. I'm so grateful to the wonderful owner of the building.

Who is your role model or mentor?
Judith Lasater, the authority on restorative yoga. She's so real and lives her yoga in the most down-to-earth way.

What is your indulgence?
A ritual we call "R&R" on Fridays: a restorative class at the studio followed by yummy pizza at Red Rocks.

Main photo (this page) by Sherry L. Brukbacher, bottom left and right photos (opposite) page by Katie Jett, portrait and bottom middle photo (opposite page) by Sian Miranda Singh ÓFaoláin

QUIET MIND YOGA

3423 14th St, NW, Washington, 202.299.0111
quietminddc.com, Twitter: @quiet_mind_yoga

Inviting. Invigorating. Inspiring.

Quiet Mind Yoga is Columbia Heights' first yoga studio, offering a thoughtful reprieve from one's daily routine by providing mindful yoga instruction in an inviting and comfortable environment. Classes focus on proper posture alignment, strengthening and fluid movement found in Iyengar, Ashtanga, and Vinyasa. The earth-friendly studio places great emphasis on the need to relax and restore, leaving students invigorated and radiating peace.

RA REDOES ROOMS

240.423.1732
rarooms.com, Twitter: @radecor

Creative. Clever. Convenient.

Ra reDoes rooms is a creative interior decorating and home-staging company, helping realtors sell homes faster and homeowners "break out of their beige haze." They help local homeowners solve home comfort challenges, specializing in custom blinds and shades for their windows.

Roslyn Ashford

Q&A

What are your most popular products or services?
Staging, color consultations, and furniture shopping.

People may be surprised to know...
While in business school, I became a founding member of a national organization of socially responsible business students and alumni, known today as Net Impact.

What business mistake have you made that you will not repeat?
Expecting other people to build my business for me. I was basically throwing my money away!

What or who inspired you to start your business?
My creative family! My grandmother was a quilter and farmer, my aunt Gloria was a master seamstress, my parents ran a business during my childhood, and my brother is a visual artist and shoe designer.

Amy Rutherford

Q&A

People may be surprised to know...
We are also committed to the environment
and stock many eco-friendly products. What's
more reused and recycled than antiques?

Who is your role model or mentor?
My parents. They are kind, compassionate,
generous, unpretentious, and full of
integrity. Those are the qualities I strive
to build in my business and my life.

What business mistake have you
made that you will not repeat?
If I could start over again, I would have better
managed my cash flow, expenses, and buying.

Where is your favorite place to
go with your girlfriends?
Dinner. For me, food is a great common
denominator and a wonderful thing to
share with people you care about.

RED BARN MERCANTILE

113 S Columbus St, Alexandria, 703.838.0355
redbarnmercantile.com, Twitter: @RedBarnMerc

Casual. Comfortable. Complete.
Red Barn Mercantile opened its doors in 2007 with a single vision in mind:
providing old and new to offer signature whole-room designs at great prices.
They work hard to bring you the highest quality furniture and gifts, the most
unique conversation starters, wall hangings and accent pieces, whether
they come from off-the-beaten-track flea markets, or the latest designers.

Photos by Meredith Rizzo Photography

Kristina Bouweiri

 # Q&A

What are your most popular
products or services?
New York shopping trips, weddings, sightseeing,
wine-country tours, airport transportation, mini-
bus shuttles, bar crawls, and scavenger hunts.

People may be surprised to know...
Reston Limousine is a major
supporter of area charities.

How do you spend your free time?
Traveling, photography, tennis, wine-
tasting events, and anything that involves
my four children and my husband.

What is your indulgence?
A massage once a week.

What do you CRAVE? In business? In life?
In business, I crave consistency and
predictability. In life, I crave balance.

Photos by Gunnar Larson

📞 RESTON LIMOUSINE
💲 AND TRAVEL SERVICE

45685 Elmwood Court, Dulles, 703.478.0500
restonlimo.com, Twitter: @restonlimo

Quality. Diversified. Service-oriented.
Founded in 1990, Reston Limousine is the largest provider of shuttle
and luxury transportation in the Washington DC area. Reston Limousine
transports government employees, university students, and staff; serves
the hospitality and tourism industry; and assists private citizens with
weddings, wine-country tours, excursions, and business transportation.

Miss Pixie's furnishings & whatnot...
photographed by Ezra Gregg

What is your indulgence?

"*I always believe in giving second chances.*"

Semra Tanrikulu of Semra Skin Care

RYAN'S AGENCY FOR MODELS

301.356.7689
ryansagencyformodels.com, Twitter: @ryansagency

Fashionable. Elegant. Professional.
Ryan's Agency for Models is a full-service modeling agency promoting
models in the areas of high fashion, runway, print, editorial, and commercial
work, with a goal of providing guidance, support, and honesty in order
to attain success in the modeling industry. Ryan's Agency for Models
upholds its mission by exposing models nationally and internationally.

Leslie Rogers

Q&A

What or who inspired you to start your business?
Aside from my love of fashion modeling,
my son has been a major inspiration for
my decision to start my own business.

Who is your role model or mentor?
My mentor was my late brother,
Kenny, who succumbed to a tragic
death. I think his determination and
endurance lives on through me.

Where is your favorite place to
go with your girlfriends?
I love to get mani-pedis with my
girlfriends. Due to our busy schedules,
this allows us quiet time together.

What do you CRAVE? In business? In life?
I crave success in business. In life,
I crave the ability to be a positive
influence within the fashion industry.

SAGE INTERIORS

703.437.0558
sageinteriors.com

Livable. Luxurious. Comfortable.

SAGE Interiors works with exclusive clientele, providing them with an array of interior design services including paint color selection and color consultations; customization of floor and architectural plans for new homes, additions, and renovations; furniture rearranging, selection, and purchasing; and window treatments and accessorizing. Owner Gwen Seidlitz specializes in creating a livable, luxury lifestyle for her clients from clean and contemporary to traditional with a twist.

Gwen Seidlitz

 Q&A

What or who inspired you to start your business?
My father is a psychiatrist and my mother is an artist. I think this fostered my creativity, thus both of my parents inspired me to start my own business.

What business mistake have you made that you will not repeat?
When I first started, I made the mistake of not taking measurements for an armoire and subsequently found that it wouldn't fit up the stairs. I can now safely say, I always take measurements.

How do you spend your free time?
I take my dog for walks. I like to spend time with family and friends. I also enjoy reading.

What do you CRAVE? In business? In life?
I crave happiness and passion for what I do, particularly helping people love their spaces.

SAINT-GERMAIN

439 7th St NW, Washington, 202.824.0444
saintgermainsalon.com

Modern. Innovative. Inspirational.
Saint-Germain's environment is a brilliant collision of influences—from the modern to the Baroque—that suffuse the salon with vitality and energy. They have cultivated an expertise and philosophical outlook that are imbued into every element of the salon. This sense of confidence and insight is the true essence of Saint-Germain.

Photos by Troy of Ex Voto Studio

Teri Ku

Q&A

What or who inspired you to start your business?
My husband, Franck. We both appreciate and are passionate about good design.

Who is your role model or mentor?
Philippe Starck, brilliant design icon. I love his vision and creativity. The design and imagination brought to life in Saint-Germain was inspired by Philippe Starck.

How do you spend your free time?
Quality time with my family.

What is your indulgence?
Interior design, traveling, and handbags.

What do you CRAVE? In business? In life?
In business, I would love to get into modern home design and handbag design. In life, I'd like more free time to travel around the world.

Jennifer Jones

 Q&A

People may be surprised to know...
Bahasa Indonesian was my first language,
and I collect vintage cowboy boots.

What or who inspired you to start your business?
It seemed I was always on the hunt for that
perfect bag, so I decided to design it.

Who is your role model or mentor?
Bali-based jeweler John Hardy, for his artistic
vision and sustainable business model. He has
embraced the Indonesian cluture and works
tirelessly to give back to the community.

How do you spend your free time?
Pop-culture exploration, not reading
instruction manuals, wondering why shoes
made for skateboarding are called Vans,
and waking up in the middle of the night
to sketch the newest SAYA design.

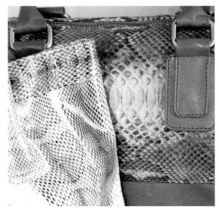

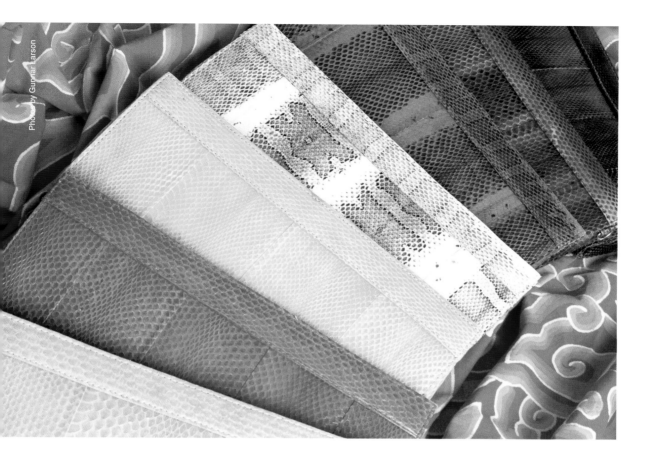

SAYA ORIGINALS

202.491.5580
sayaoriginals.com

Classic. Sassy. Original.

SAYA Originals creates snakeskin purses and accessories. Raised in Indonesia,
owner Jennifer Jones has spent much time in the same toko (small shop) where
her mom had things made in the 1970s. Her goal with SAYA Originals is to create
chic, timeless pieces that will someday cause your granddaughter to exclaim,
"Can I borrow this?" and give a little something back to a country she loves.

Semra
Tanrikulu

Q&A

What or who inspired you to start your business?
I love to work with people one-on-one
to bring out their best and give them
confidence. Sometimes a little eyebrow
job can make a big difference!

Who is your role model or mentor?
My role model in life is my father. He
is a very hard worker and has a strong
personality with a big heart.

**Where is your favorite place to
go with your girlfriends?**
POV at the W Hotel for the best view,
Peacock Cafe for the best burgers, and Maté
for great sushi and lounge atmosphere.

What do you CRAVE? In business? In life?
I most desire to see my name become a
brand for a line of beauty products, and I
would also like to open a beauty school.

SEMRA SKIN CARE

3109 M St NW, Ste 300, Washington, 202.342.0944
semra4skin.com

Glamorous. Magical. Fresh.
Owner Semra Tanrikulu has been an aesthetician for more than 15
years. Well known for her award-winning eyebrows, she is also an
expert in facials, eyelash extensions, makeup, and spray tanning. She
has worked for Chanel for eight years as an eyebrow specialist and was
featured in the *Washingtonian* magazine's "best of Georgetown."

Georgetown

THE SHOE HIVE

127 S Fairfax St, Alexandria, 703.548.7105
theshoehive.com

Classic. Personalized. Elegant.

The Shoe Hive is a well-regarded women's shoe boutique in the heart of historic Old Town Alexandria. It features a fashionable collection of shoes and bags from the best brands and undiscovered designers, all delivered with pampering personal service.

Elizabeth Todd

Q&A

What or who inspired you to start your business?
Three of the most ignorant people when it
comes to women's shoes: my old boss Sam
Van Voorhis, my husband, and my father.
They all fostered my entrepreneurial spirit and
have supported me since I opened in 2003.

Who is your role model or mentor?
My grandmother Butcher. She
is full of sass and class.

What business mistake have you
made that you will not repeat?
I wasn't open on certain holidays my first few
years. Now they are some of my best days.

Where is your favorite place to
go with your girlfriends?
Grape + Bean in Old Town.

lillybee

Kassie Rempel

Q&A

What are your most popular products or services?
The lillybee line which I design, our extensive Tory Burch collection, and our exclusive styles from designers such as Bettye Muller, Chie Mihara, Missoni, and more.

People may be surprised to know...
I started my career as a CPA, which, thanks to the drab work attire (suits in gray, navy, or black), ignited a love of shoes, bags, and necklaces.

What business mistake have you made that you will not repeat?
Overhiring. If a person isn't performing, they need to be let go. It's hard to do in small companies because it affects morale, but it's best for the business and the staff in the long run.

SIMPLYSOLES

3222 M St NW, 2nd Floor, Washington, 202.232.0072
Twitter: @simplysoles

Stylish. Inviting. Unique.
SimplySoles carries stylish shoes, unique handbags, and playful jewelry. Having successfully operated an online boutique and popular print catalog for more than five years, SimplySoles just opened their first brick-and-mortar store in Georgetown. Carrying an array of exclusive designs, including Kassie's own line—lillybee—SimplySoles caters to the stylish woman looking for the unique.

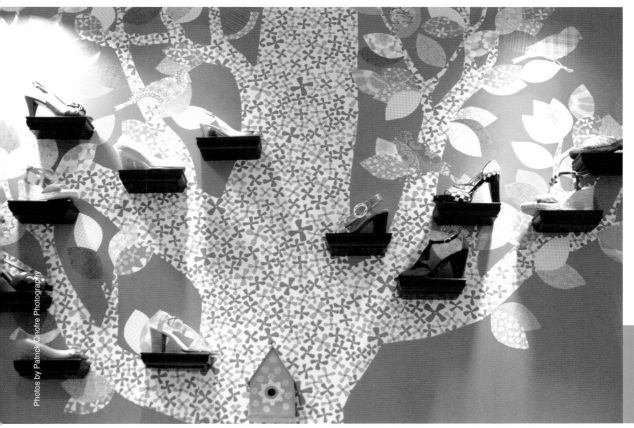

Photos by Patrick Onofre Photography

Georgetown

Sissy Yates

 # Q & A

What or who inspired you to start your business?
I have always made jewelry for friends and family. A few years ago, my sister (Ali Wentworth Stephanopoulos) told me it was time to go public. She hosted my first show at her home and sold everything in two hours.

People may be surprised to know...
I have been collecting rocks since I was five years old.

Who is your role model or mentor?
Friends who have achieved the American Dream.

Where is your favorite place to go with your girlfriends?
Hiking in Battery Kemble Park with our dogs.

What do you CRAVE? In business? In life?
I crave adventure, new challenges, success and, of course, beautiful and rare stones.

SISSY YATES DESIGNS

202.262.2834
sissyyatesdesigns.com

Classical. Stylish. One-of-a-kind.
Sissy Yates Designs specializes in the creation of affordable, stylish, and unique jewelry made from rare and colorful stones from around the world. The necklaces, earrings, and bracelets are sold in retail stores across the country, and have been featured in national publications such as the *Washington Post* and *O Magazine*. Local retail stores include Sherman Pickey, Upstairs on 7th, and Après Peau.

SISTERS & SUCH
SANDWICH BOUTIQUE

16834 Georgia Ave, Olney, 301.774.0669

Funky. Creative. Delicious.
Sisters & Such Sandwich Boutique is just what Olney, Maryland needed!
They feature mouth-watering sandwiches, salads, and soups made from the
freshest ingredients—breads, quality meats, cheeses, herbs, and spreads.
Sisters is well known for their funky salvage furniture available in-store and
their array of made-in-the-United-States, recyclable, vintage gifts.

Tammy Prestipino and Kim Carlson

Q&A

What are your most popular products or services?
Our dine-in or carry-out sandwiches and salads are to die for.

How do you spend your free time?
Tammy: with my three girls, on the lake, walking the dog, hanging with my husband, or painting. Kim: working in the yard, sewing, and planning vacations.

Where is your favorite place to go with your girlfriends?
The lake house at Lake Anna with the girls.

What do you CRAVE? In business? In life?
Pleasing people and showing our faith in all that we do.

Who is your role model or mentor?
Our crazy mother, Ruth—we miss her dearly. She taught us how to laugh and see the good in everything.

SKINCANDO

202.215.8991
skincando.com, Twitter: @skincando

Superior. Beautiful. Organic.
Skincando is a unique organic skin-care company. They handcraft skin-beautifying
products with 100 percent high-quality organic and wild-crafted ingredients.
As a sustainable company, they work at eliminating their carbon footprint and
believe in giving. They purchase local ingredients, use non-toxic cleansers
and organic bamboo cloths in their production process, and bio-recycle.

Sara Damelio

Q&A

People may be surprised to know...
Skincando has set up a not-for-profit
charity called Operation Sand Flea. On
our website, clients can donate discounted
Combat-Ready Balm to send to US troops
stationed abroad. Skincando sends the
products in care packages with thank-you
notes and covers the shipping expense.

What or who inspired you to start your business?
My own problem skin and the inability to
find beauty products that actually worked.

How do you spend your free time?
"There is a time for work and a time for love.
That leaves no other time."—Coco Chanel

Where is your favorite place to
go with your girlfriends?
The Still Point in Takoma Park, Maryland.

Lena Johnson, Maria Moreno, and Natalie Moreno

Q&A

People may be surprised to know...
We are family-owned—a mother-daughter-cousin team!

What or who inspired you to start your business?
Our homes are the primary hub for our large family gatherings. Starting a business doing something that we enjoy just made sense.

Where is your favorite place to go with your girlfriends?
Anywhere with good food, good music, and a dance floor!

What do you CRAVE? In business? In life?
Positivity. It brings balance and productivity and with these you can achieve anything.

☎ THE SOCIAL

202.642.9011, 202.642.9012
thesocialllc.com, Twitter: @TheSocialLLC

Innovative. Modern. Refined.
The Social is a team of creative planning consultants offering complete event management. They bring exciting and fresh ideas to their clients, creating truly unforgettable experiences. With attention to detail and tailored packages, their true value is in the complete quality of their services. Whether you're looking to host a corporate dinner or simply add sparkle to a private party, The Social will make the difference.

Photos by Eddie Paylor except upper right photo (opposite page)

Dana Smith-Rogers

 Q&A

People may be surprised to know...
Yoga can be practiced by anyone,
regardless of age or ability.

Who is your role model or mentor?
My father is my role model! He's been an
entrepreneur for more than 40 years and gives
me sage advice on how to run my business.

What business mistake have you
made that you will not repeat?
When I first started, I priced myself too low in
order to get more clients. I wound up with more
clients than I could handle and burned out.

How do you spend your free time?
I love to read, take walks with my family,
and experiment with new healthy recipes.

What is your indulgence?
I just *love* dark chocolate.

Photos by Meredith Rizzo Photography

SPIRITUAL ESSENCE
YOGA & WELLNESS CENTER

13100 Brooke Lane, Upper Marlboro, 301.574.FLOW (3569)
spiritualessenceyoga.com, Twitter: @se_yoga

Enlightening. Relaxing. Organic.
Spiritual Essence Yoga & Wellness Center specializes in yoga, meditation, dance, and creative movement classes for every*body*. For those needing a great escape, they offer relaxing holistic wellness therapies that include Thai yoga bodywork, Reiki, and essential herbal body wraps. In addition to classes and wellness therapies, Spiritual Essence Yoga also offers training and certification programs.

181

STANTON GALLERY

121 S Royal St, 2nd floor, Alexandria, 703.299.3055
stantonjewelry.com, Twitter: @stantongallery

Personal. Creative. Sophisticated.
Stanton Gallery is one of Alexandria's hidden gems. Specializing in one-of-a-kind custom jewelry, Stanton Gallery offers a private setting in which to work directly with owner Christine Stanton. Clients are involved in the wonderful process of designing that special piece of jewelry, whether it be for an engagement, a wedding, or just turning an old piece in your jewelry box into something new!

Christine Stanton

 Q&A

People may be surprised to know...
I do my best creative work between
the hours of 12am and 4am.

Who is your role model or mentor?
My amazing parents. They have always
been there to support my creativity and
encourage me to be the best that I can be.

How do you spend your free time?
With my wonderful husband and
our two amazing little girls.

What is your indulgence?
A great bottle of red wine from GRAPE+BEAN.

Where is your favorite place to
go with your girlfriends?
Weekend sailing trips to St. Michaels.

Tori Paide

Q&A

What are your most popular products or services?
Therapeutic massage, holistic skin care, acupuncture, and eco-makeup.

Where is your favorite place to go with your girlfriends?
Their houses for a long, drawn-out dinner and lots of great conversation.

Who is your role model or mentor?
A former supervisor who recently passed away after a long journey with cancer. She was a tough businesswoman who stayed centered and graceful.

How do you spend your free time?
With my kids and husband.

What is your indulgence?
Spa treatments!

THE STILL POINT

1 Columbia Ave, Takoma Park, 301.920.0801
stillpointmindandbody.com, Twitter: @thestillpoint

Natural. Invigorating. Serene.
A truly holistic spa, The Still Point's full range of services are tailored to support
and enable clients to live their best lives right here, right now. They offer services
ranging from acupuncture and therapeutic massage to non-toxic pedicures
and organic facials, all provided in a modern space of tranquility and peace.

Portrait by Patrick Onofre Photography

Diva Designer Consignment & Other Delights
photographed by Meredith Rizzo Photography

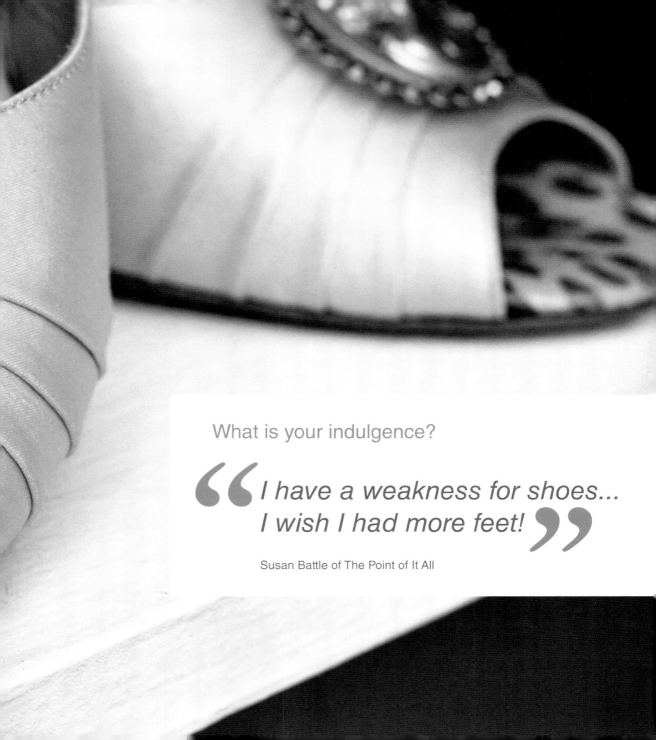

What is your indulgence?

*" I have a weakness for shoes...
I wish I had more feet! "*

Susan Battle of The Point of It All

Studio 310

Liz Corah

Q&A

People may be surprised to know:
The studio is my oasis. The walls of my kitchen and family room (at home) were subconsciously painted the same colors as the studio.

What or who inspired you to start your business?
My pseudo-sister, Jennifer Kaye, who one day asked, "What are you doing with your life?"

Who is your role model or mentor?
Angie Bunch (founder of Culture Shock), Erin Brockovich, Maya Angelou, Coco Chanel, and my grandmother, Sheila Sobel. I am also inspired every day by the people around me.

What is your indulgence?
Daydreaming. I have been a daydreamer since I was a little girl. I can completely zone out from the world around me and go wherever I want. It's helped me come up with some of my best ideas.

STUDIO-310

$

9743 Traville Gateway Drive, Rockville, 301.838.0310
studio-310.com, Twitter: @LizCorah

Motivational. Fun. Inspiring.

Studio-310 is a unique place where fitness and dance blend to inspire people of all ages to feel, look, and be their best. From ballet to boot camp, offerings are designed to build strength, endurance, and confidence that members take with them long after they leave the studio. Their mantras include "Confidence is Beauty," "Strong is the new Thin," and "Just Dance."

SUCCESS IN THE CITY

1430 Spring Hill Road, Ste 575, McLean, 202.747.1782 x100
successinthecity.org, Twitter: @SuccessntheCity

Superstar. Accomplished. Successful.
Success in the City serves women who stand out, lead, and influence
others. Their objective is to help members develop lasting peer
relationships with other successful women. Trust and humor are key
elements for women in developing lasting friendships, and once those
relationships are formed, deals-on-heels are sure to follow!

Photos by Success in the City, except portrait by Patrick Onofre Photography

Cynthia de Lorenzi

Q&A

People may be surprised to know...
Success in the City events and programs
are developed based on actual studies
related to women and stress.

What or who inspired you to start your business?
Girlfriend bankruptcy was the inspiration and
catalyst for creating Success in the City. After
moving to Washington DC, I found that it was
difficult to find other women leaders like myself.
I wanted to connect on a personal level and
develop those meaningful friendships that
sustain us as we face the challenges of busy
lives and successful growing companies.

What do you CRAVE? In business? In life?
In business, taking Success in the City
international with chapters in major
cities around the world. In life, having
time to relax and enjoy my family!

Kimberly Wilson

Q&A

What are your most popular products or services?
Inspiring yoga classes, yummy spa services, stylish organic clothing, and green gifts—particularly glittery cards, reusable water bottles, and eco yoga mats.

People may be surprised to know...
Tranquil Space started in my living room in 1999 and has a sister nonprofit, Tranquil Space Foundation.

What or who inspired you to start your business?
A desire to create community, meet like-minded people, and make a difference.

Who is your role model or mentor?
I'm inspired by Martha Stewart, Melinda Gates, and Madonna.

TRANQUIL SPACE

1632 17th St NW, Washington, 202.328.9642
3528 Wilson Blvd, Arlington, 703.348.7993
tranquilspace.com, Twitter: @tranquilspace

Nurturing. Inspiring. Holistic.

Tranquil Space is a lifestyle-focused yoga destination named among the top 25 yoga studios in the world. They offer more than 50 creative classes weekly in their sunny studios. Sip organic tea and shop the tranquility boutique filled with green gifts. Indulge in their specialty spa offering massages, Reiki, ayurvedic consultations, and more. Uncover your own tranquil space within.

Photos by Meredith Rizzo Photography

TREAT

103 S St. Asaph St, Alexandria, 703.535.3294
shoptreat.com, Twitter: @shoptreat

Sleek. Savvy. Unique.
The first and only shop of its kind in the DC area, Treat brings a fresh perspective to discount shopping by offering favorite designer brands at sample sale prices in a boutique setting. Treat features a highly edited selection of clothing, shoes, handbags, and jewelry, all marked down to as much as 80 percent off retail, in a bright and airy boutique in historic Old Town.

Jennifer Donohue

 Q&A

What are your most popular
products or services?
Handbags and dresses are always best-sellers,
but jewelry and denim are also very popular.

Who is your role model or mentor?
A few of my girlfriends who also happen to be
fellow entrepreneurs and amazing women.

How do you spend your free time?
Enjoying family and friends, eating good
food, and taking Pilates classes.

What do you CRAVE? In business? In life?
A sense of accomplishment and happiness.

What is your indulgence?
Mani/pedis and the occasional massage.

What or who inspired you to start your business?
My love for fashion and discount
shopping and a frustration with the
lack of options in the DC area.

TWINS JAZZ CLUB

1344 U St NW, Top Floor, Washington, 202.234.0072
twinsjazz.com, Twitter: @twinsjazzclub

Authentic. Lively. Jazzy.

Serving the District for more than 20 years, Twins Jazz offers its own atmospheric vibe—a hip spot for great international food, creative cocktails, and live music nightly. The club features contemporary lighting, a colored ceramic cavelike bar, an action-packed stage, and story-telling photography. Styled for music enthusiasts and art lovers, Twins Jazz is a great place to make memories.

Maze Tesfaye,
Love-leigh Beasley, and Kelly Tesfaye

Q&A

What are your most popular
products or services?
Live jazz every day of the week and
Ethiopian/American/Caribbean cuisine.

People may be surprised to know...
Twins Jazz is owned and operated by real-life
twin sisters, Kelly and Maze Tesfaye, along with
their daughter and niece, Love-leigh Beasley.

Who is your role model or mentor?
Love-leigh: my mother and aunt—the Twins!

How do you spend your free time?
Nonprofit work with The Twins Jazz Foundation
(TwinsJazz.org) and TheCollegeAdvocate.org.

What do you CRAVE? In business? In life?
Twins Jazz achieving landmark
status in Washington DC.

U Street

Melanie Smith Jones

 # Q&A

People may be surprised to know...
I was 23 when I started Urban Style Lab.

What or who inspired you to start your business?
My dad encouraged me to do it, despite
my age. I trusted him, since he started his
business when he was in his 20s as well!

Where is your favorite place to
go with your girlfriends?
We love to try out the new restaurants of DC,
and travel together to Vegas, NYC, and Miami.

What do you CRAVE? In business? In life?
Staff and client satisfaction in business, and
quality time with my family and friends in life.

Who is your role model or mentor?
Remi Metsu, owner of Salon180, who
I trained under. I can always count on
him to give me helpful advice.

Dupont Circle

URBAN STYLE LAB

$

1341 Connecticut Ave NW, Ste 1, Washington, 202.223.2066
lab-dc.com, Twitter: @urbanstylelab

Vibrant. Hip. Friendly.
Five years ago Melanie Smith Jones came to DC's Dupont Circle with one
mission: to craft beautiful looks and leave nothing but stylish, healthy hair
in her wake. She has since crafted a team at Urban Style Lab that works to
create a relaxed environment focused on modern, fashion-forward hair.

VALERIANNE

111 Church St NW, Ste 201, Vienna, 703.242.1790
valerianne.com, Twitter: @valerianne

Luxurious. Current. Distinctive.

Valerianne is a luxury home finishings boutique featuring a truly exclusive range of the finest available for table, bed, bath, and home. The shop is filled with beautifully appointed luxury items and found objects that reflect today's eclectic lifestyles. Valerianne is proud to offer products that will withstand the test of time but also embrace the feel of the moment.

Aimee Wedlake Lange

Q&A

People may be surprised to know...
When we put a bed together for you, part of our service is delivering it to your home freshly pressed and assembled just as you saw it in the showroom. We ensure everything fits the way it is supposed to and is exactly what you envisioned. Sweet dreams!

What business mistake have you made that you will not repeat?
Making promises and commitments that are impossible to keep. I am guilty of trying to make everyone happy and satisfied. I constantly remind myself there are only so many hours in each day and it's impossible to please everyone.

What is your indulgence?
Doing something by myself. My business is all about the wonderful relationships that I create with my clients. I enjoy everyone I meet but it is a true indulgence to be able to be totally quiet and sit with my thoughts or a good book, or even treat myself to a pedicure.

Vienna

Deborah E. Myers

 # Q&A

People may be surprised to know...
There are artisans around the globe
creating beautiful works of art, utilizing
techniques unknown to us but passed
down from generation to generation.

What or who inspired you to start your business?
The desire to help artists/artisans in the
developing world market their unique,
beautiful work to a global audience.

Who is your role model or mentor?
My role model is Natalie Massenet,
founder of Net-a-Porter.

How do you spend your free time?
I spend my free time reading, doing jigsaw
puzzles, and watching old movies on TCM.

VIRTUARTE

virtuarte.com, Twitter: @VirtuArte

Dynamic. Global. Creative.

VirtuArte discovers handcrafted art, folk art, fine crafts, and curios in the developing world and sells these pieces to an international clientele. VirtuArte helps artisans from around the globe generate sustainable incomes to support their families, improve the quality of their lives, continue their traditional craftsmanship, and pass their skills on to the next generation.

VM PHOTOGRAPHY & MAKEUP STUDIO

5700 Baltimore Ave, Hyattsville, 301.367.8739
Available on location in the Washington DC area
vmarkelou.com, thethriftyfashionista.com

Creative. Beautiful. Empowered.

VM Photography & Makeup Studio is a one-stop shopping destination
for elegant and bold photography with an expertise in beauty and style. VM
Photography & Makeup Studio possesses the ability to capture a mood using
innovation and creativity while offering each subject a relaxed environment.
Keeping a close eye to beauty and fashion trends, VM Photography & Makeup
Studio aspires to create timeless images and beauty for each client.

Main photo (this page) by Dave Ruff; top left, middle, and right photos (opposite page) by Violetta Markelou; portrait (opposite page) by Yassine Elmansouri

Violetta Markelou

Q&A

What or who inspired you to start your business?
Knowing that there *is* a way to make your dreams of independence come true. Knowing that you *absolutely can* do what you love and create a lucrative career.

People may be surprised to know...
I'm a drugstore junkie! I love CVS and Rite Aid and use coupons! Almost all of the beauty and skin care products I recommend to clients can be found in the drugstore.

Who is your role model or mentor?
I am inspired on a daily basis by many people in my life as well as a few public figures— Tom Ford and Annie Leibovitz to name a few—who have demonstrated to me that you can create a dream career with pure ambition, fearlessness, and positive thinking.

Photos by Meredith Rizzo Photography, except bottom left photo (opposite page) by Paul Butterfield Photography

WARMLY, ALEYSHA

301.523.7389
aleyshaproctor.com, Twitter: @AleyshaProctor

Inspirational. Elegant. Cultural.

Aleysha Proctor is a Christian inspirational author and speaker in the DC metro area. Her work has been described as life changing and motivating. She inspires you to use your potential *now* and change your perspective. She also writes an inspirational blog.

Aleysha Proctor

 # Q&A

What or who inspired you to start your business?
I have an enterprising mindset, so it only made sense to parlay my talents into a business that could help others.

People may be surprised to know...
I'm actually pretty shy.

Who is your role model or mentor?
My grandmother, mother, and sister are my role models. They're all wonderful women.

What business mistake have you made that you will not repeat?
In the past, I have spent excessive amounts of money on ineffective advertising. The world of advertising has truly changed for the better.

Where is your favorite place to go with your girlfriends?
The National Harbor in Maryland—hands down!

Intelligentsia

Business-to-business entreprenesses, including coaching, marketing, and public relations, photography, business consulting, and design services.

2HEARTS CONSULTING

540.220.1789
2heartsllc.com, Twitter: @2heartsllc

Strategic. Transformational. Quantum.
Founded by Joan Greback Clarke, 2Hearts Consulting provides strategic development solutions in the areas of marketing, planning, and implementation of transformational giving and mega-gift programs, as well as capital and special gift campaigns, board governance, strategic planning, and management. 2Hearts specializes in moving organizations to new levels of sustained growth and financial stability through enhanced giving programs.

Photo by Bill Buttram Photography

Joan Greback Clarke

 Q&A

Who is your role model or mentor?
Two Mother Teresas—my mother, Teresa Greback, and the Blessed Mother Teresa of Calcutta. They are both the epitome of service. Service is hard work, and with hard work comes love. Love truly changes the world.

What or who inspired you to start your business?
2Hearts was the brainchild of a collective thought to give more than you should take. Two decades ago I developed a system of linking the heart of the donor with the heart of the institution, one relationship at a time. Our nonprofit clients now have a more faithful and strategic way to secure major gifts. By using their heart and soul, our 2Hearts team creates the right mix of art and science to make our clients successful.

BLISK FINANCIAL

Located at Spire Investment Partners:
7918 Jones Branch Drive, Ste 750, McLean, 703.748.5800
spireip.com

Trustworthy. Experienced. Unbiased.
Blisk Financial specializes in helping families navigate through
significant life changes, such as career transition, divorce, business
succession, and widowhood. With an independent financial planning
team of licensed professionals, and more than 80 years of combined
experience, clients receive sound advice and guidance when
making strategic financial and investment decisions. Blisk Financial
provides a disciplined, proactive approach to financial planning.

Brenda Blisk

 Q&A

People may be surprised to know...
I grew up on a Tennessee dairy farm and
milked cows before going to school each day...
no better way to develop a strong work ethic!

What or who inspired you to start your business?
Having a desire to make a meaningful difference
in the lives of my friends, family, and clients.

What business mistake have you
made that you will not repeat?
Trying to serve clients for whom we were
not a good match. I've learned that you
cannot be all things to all people.

What do you CRAVE? In business? In life?
The satisfaction of knowing that I have
made a valuable contribution. This
gives me true, heartfelt fulfillment.

CHIC COMMUNICATIONS

chicpr.com, Twitter: @ChicPRDC

Fresh. Successful. Fabulous.
Founded in 2009, Chic Communications is a boutique firm focusing on public relations, marketing, special events, and social media outreach. Their expertise deals with fashion, beauty, luxury lifestyle, and corporate image.

Morgan McLoud and Kristin McMahon

 Q&A

What are your most popular products or services?
Public relations, marketing, and special events.

People may be surprised to know...
Combined, we have assisted with more than 300 events in the DC metro area.

What business mistake have you made that you will not repeat?
Not realizing sooner that if you embrace your passion, success will follow.

How do you spend your free time?
Morgan enjoys traveling, spending time on her boat cruising the Chesapeake Bay, and having fun with her Maltese, Cosmopolitan. Kristin is an active member of the Junior League of Northern Virginia and loves to play with her Teacup Yorkie, Louis (yes, as in Louis Vuitton).

CREATIVE BLOG SOLUTIONS

301.421.4183
creativeblogsolutions.com, Twitter: @creativeblogs

Progressive. Creative. Impact-driven.
Creative Blog Solutions works with businesses that understand the value of leveraging emerging technology to build deep relationships with prospects, customers, and constituents. Creative Blog Solutions helps clients use the social web to build brand authority, generate high-quality leads, and increase market share.

Terri Holley

 **Q&A**

What are your most popular products or services?
Social media campaign development and management, business blogs, and Facebook fan page design and "how-to" training.

What or who inspired you to start your business?
My strong desire to help other business owners develop a thorough understanding of how to use social media to market their business. No one should be left in the dark!

What is your indulgence?
Any technological tool that makes my life more efficient or more interesting. Apple has got to love me!

What do you CRAVE? In business? In life?
Excellence, creativity, and the freedom to just be me.

213

ECO-COACH

202.559.0777
eco-coach.com, Twitter: @ecocoach

Ecological. Sustainable. Solutions-oriented.
Eco-Coach is a WBENC and CBE-certified sustainability advisory firm. Started in 2006, Eco-Coach assists individuals and businesses in going green, and helps them save money and have fun while doing it. Eco-Coach offers a variety of services to suit different needs and varying levels of 'green' awareness. Services for individuals include workshops and home eco-audits. For businesses, Eco-Coach's focus is on "greening" business operations, training and education, and green building support.

Anca Novacovici

Photo by Jeremy Bigwood

 Q&A

What are your most popular products or services?
For individuals, educational workshops and home eco-audits. For businesses, eco-assessments and workshops on energy efficiency, carbon footprinting, waste management, etc.

Who is your role model or mentor?
Too many to list! For entrepreneurship, it is Richard Branson.

What business mistake have you made that you will not repeat?
Offering too many types of services at once. I learned that it is important to identify your strengths and your passion, then pick a niche to focus on.

How do you spend your free time?
Outdoors whenever possible, and with friends and family. Some new hobbies include horseback riding and Argentine tango.

EVOLUTION CONSULTING GROUP

301.681.1438
evolutionconsultinggroup.com, Twitter: @ECGMarketing

Creative. Resourceful. Dynamic.
Evolution Consulting Group is a marketing consulting company committed to helping its clients evolve their businesses to the next level. Dedicated to providing innovative and creative marketing solutions that generate exceptional results, Evolution Consulting Group uses expertise in marketing to illuminate pathways, open doors, and guide businesses toward growth. Services include marketing consultation, brand marketing, event marketing, and strategic alliances.

Photo by Roy Cox Photography

Wendy McAllister

 Q&A

What are your most popular products or services?
Marketing plans and strategies that help my clients to achieve their business goals.

What or who inspired you to start your business?
The desire to have some freedom over what I was doing professionally. I wanted to be doing work that was fulfilling, aligned with my interests and passions, and helped others to evolve their businesses to the next level.

Who is your role model or mentor?
Oprah is one of my role models. She's a smart, successful businesswoman who has built a global brand that has positively impacted the lives of millions.

What is your indulgence?
Spa treatments! Cupcakes! Fine cuisine!

THE INSPIRED OFFICE

202.262.1207
theinspiredoffice.com, Twitter: @kacypaide

Creative. Personalized. Detailed.
Kacy Paide works with creative business owners who are desperate for a
more organized, beautiful, inspiring office. She works with clients who used
to think they were too creative to ever be organized. Kacy's custom-designed
paper-flow systems can be found all across paper-filled Washington DC. If
her clients can find what they need when they need it, her work is done.

Photo by Tazima Davis

Kacy Paide

 Q&A

What are your most popular
products or services?
Most clients have a relationship with paper that
is "out-of-sight, out-of-mind," so I'm often asked
to create alternatives to traditional filing systems.

People may be surprised to know...
How intensely therapeutic it feels to
release years' worth of old papers in
a matter of minutes or hours.

What business mistake have you
made that you will not repeat?
Not carving out a niche years earlier. That single
decision immediately transformed my business.

What or who inspired you to start your business?
My study abroad trip to Bali inspired
me not only to work for myself, but also
to make a living creating beauty.

INVISION

301.654.5293
invisionllc.com

Connecting. Engaging. Inspiring.
InVision helps leaders thrive, offer tangible value, and get results. They listen carefully to clients' needs and customize their consulting and coaching approach to address clients' personal and professional challenges. Clients learn and exercise the best practices of leadership to achieve their goals and engage their people. After a dozen years in business, clients repeatedly report they are passionate, engaged, and flourishing as a result of working with them.

Photo by Meaghan Farren-Smith

Heather Kaye

 Q&A

What are your most popular products or services?
Individual and team leadership coaching and consulting. The Leadership Sanctuary for nonprofit leaders.

What or who inspired you to start your business?
My dad was an entrepreneur. He had vision! He bought a three-person company teetering on bankruptcy and built it to become the largest weather-stripping company in Canada.

Who is your role model or mentor?
I have had many and one of the people who had the greatest impact was Caela Farren, founder of MasteryWorks.

What do you CRAVE? In business? In life?
In life, lots of laughs, unbridled fun, and rich, loving connections. In business, clients who are committed to manifesting their dreams.

LENA ABURDENE, MS

1317 G St NW, Washington, 703.903.9696 x217
lenamariems.wordpress.com, Twitter: @LenaMarieA

Compassionate. Insightful. Accepting.
Lena Aburdene, MS, is a resident in pastoral counseling working within an already established practice called the Center for Pastoral Counseling of Virginia. Lena uses a caring, empathic, and nonjudgmental approach and believes that compassion and acceptance are two of the most important aspects in a therapeutic relationship. Her goal is to help others embrace their true potential in order to find happiness.

Photo by Mary Elizabeth Harty

Lena Marie Aburdene

 Q&A

What are your most popular products or services?
People going through difficult life transitions or loss often seek out my services.

People may be surprised to know...
I am a food correspondent and lifestyle writer for popular Washington DC blog, Pamela's Punch (pamelaspunch.com).

Who is your role model or mentor?
Every single person who has been a client of mine is also a role model of mine. Their strength and perseverance motivate and inspire me.

How do you spend your free time?
DJing on my turntables, performing improvisational comedy, writing, emceeing events, and raising money for great causes.

LOVAS CONSULTING

lovasconsulting.com, Twitter: @jlovas

Empowering. Supportive. Motivational.
Lovas Consulting empowers SMB women-owned businesses to grow and expand while taking control of their lives. Jane Lovas's book, *Ordinary Women, Extraordinary Lives: Creating a Life of Purpose, Passion and Prosperity*, provides you with the motivation and the steps to create the life you want no matter where you currently are in life.

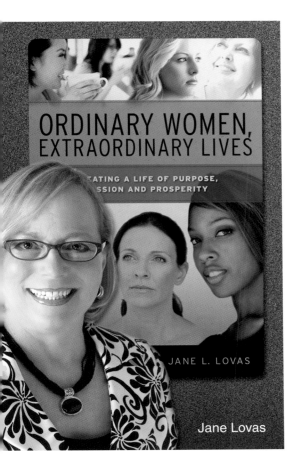

 Q&A

What are your most popular products or services?
Supporting women as they grow their business and retain their life.

People may be surprised to know...
I never planned on being an author. *Ordinary Women, Extraordinary Lives: Creating a Life of Purpose, Passion and Prosperity* had its own life for me!

How do you spend your free time?
Spending time with my girls, reading, practicing photography, and skiing.

What is your indulgence?
Getting a massage.

Who is your role model or mentor?
Helen Keller.

MEREDITH RIZZO PHOTOGRAPHY

804.868.0821
meredithrizzo.com

Focused. Photojournalistic. Versatile.
Meredith Rizzo Photography is a Washington DC–based freelance photography business specializing in editorial, photojournalistic-style photography. With a passion for environmental portraiture, Meredith provides photography for events, weddings, publications, and nonprofit organizations.

Photo by Lewis Wyman

Meredith Rizzo

Q&A

What or who inspired you to start your business?
My dad's old Canon A-1, which I still have, sparked my interest in photography.

What business mistake have you made that you will not repeat?
Buying too much equipment. It's amazing what you can do with the basics.

How do you spend your free time?
Washington DC is perfect for bike riding, seeing museums, eating, and commuting. Any free time is usually spent doing one of those.

What is your indulgence?
Books. I never have enough shelves.

What do you CRAVE? In business? In life?
I crave any type of outlet for creative energy. It helps me focus.

MERYL HOOKER,
SALES ROCKSTAR

877.277.1171
merylhooker.com, Twitter: @merylhooker

Creative. Motivational. Educational.
Meryl Hooker loves helping small businesses. She is the author of
Road Rage, a blog about repping, selling, and customer service, and
she also writes occasional columns for publication. Her first book,
*Pushing the Envelope: The Small Greeting Card Manufacturer's
Guide to Working with Sales Reps*, was launched in May 2010.

Photo by Patrick Onofre Photography

Meryl Hooker

 # Q&A

What are your most popular
products or services?
Funny always sells. I'm also getting a lot of
questions about how independent retailers can
use social networking media to drive sales.

Who is your role model or mentor?
My customers have helped the most. They've
taught me so much about being a great rep,
very little of which has to do with selling.

What or who inspired you to start your business?
I didn't want a "real job." Little did I know...

What is your indulgence?
Cupcakes, cupcakes, cupcakes!

How do you spend your free time?
I love to swing dance!

The Still Point photographed
by Patrick Onofre Photography

What do you CRAVE? In business? In life?

"Good conversation... the kind that's deep, organic, free-flowing, mind-blowing."

Summer Amin of NiMA Integrated Marketing Boutique

MOKI MEDIA

1410 Q St NW, Washington, 301.807.0910, 202.257.9911
mokimedia.com, Twitter: @mokimediapr

Personalized. Connected. Dedicated.
As a boutique public relations firm, MoKi Media provides responsive, high-quality services to boost, expand, or reinvent any business through media exposure, image consulting, and networking. With a unique combination of publishing and public relations expertise, and access to an extensive network of print, broadcast, and online media outlets, MoKi Media creates value by providing a buzz for businesses and events.

Photo by Gene Young

Sherry Moeller and Dannia Hakki

 # Q&A

What are your most popular products or services?
Public relations including media exposure, networking, and events.

Where is your favorite place to go with your girlfriends?
Sherry: We meet at Frosting Bakeshop & Coffee Bar in Chevy Chase and love sampling all the sweets.
Dannia: My friends and I go to Peacock Cafe in Georgetown where the French Kiss cocktail is better than the real thing.

What do you CRAVE? In business? In life?
In business, we both crave success, ecstatic clients, and loyalty. In life, happiness, family, and love are at the top of our lists.

$ NICOLE INDELICATO

908.216.0409
nicoleindelicato.com, Twitter: @n_indelicato

Authentic. Inspired. Empowered.
Nicole Indelicato is a success coach providing Generation Y athletes, entrepreneurs, quarter-lifers, and world changers with tools, strategies, inspiration, and empowerment. Nicole works with clients who are navigating the big questions in life by dissolving limiting beliefs and creating a workable action plan, which ultimately leads to purpose, passion, and legacy. Life is a journey and we all have a unique story to share.

Photo by Meredith Rizzo Photography

Nicole M. Indelicato

 Q&A

What are your most popular products or services?
My one-on-one laser-focused coaching sessions. It's a privilege to witness my clients' "aha" moments.

People may be surprised to know...
I'm an adventure enthusiast: I dive out of planes, I jump off bridges, and I swim with great white sharks.

Where is your favorite place to go with your girlfriends?
Tranquil Space in Dupont Circle. There is nothing better than quality girlfriend time mixed with yoga and meditation.

What is your indulgence?
Handbags and stilettos. A girl can never have too many.

NIMA INTEGRATED MARKETING BOUTIQUE

202.642.2451
nimamarketing.com, Twitter: @nimamarketing, @summeramin

Creative. Compelling. Clever.
NiMA is a one-stop shop that provides a full range of integrated marketing and communications services—from strategy to writing to design to execution—to small businesses, nonprofit organizations, and trade associations. Whether you're a new venture or an established outfit, NiMA can help you meet your goals through out-of-the-box, cost-effective print and online solutions.

Photo by Patrick Onofre Photography

Summer Amin

 # Q&A

What or who inspired you to start your business?
I realized one day that I didn't just want to make a living; I wanted to make a difference.

People may be surprised to know...
I am an extroverted introvert.

Who is your role model or mentor?
My sister. I'm so proud of her that she makes me want to be a better person—and vice versa!

How do you spend your free time?
I love to go to new places, try new foods, meet new people, and learn new things.

What do you CRAVE? In business? In life?
Good conversation... the kind that's deep, organic, free-flowing, mind-blowing.

PREAL HALEY & ASSOCIATES

7711 Belle Point Dr, Greenbelt, 301.982.1206
ameripriseadvisors.com/preal.2.haley/profile

Empowering. Urgent. Necessary.
Preal Haley has been helping people reach goals for more than 10 years.
As an independent franchise owner and financial advisor with Ameriprise
Financial Services, Inc., Preal believes success is measured not just by your
financial well-being, but by how confident you feel about your future. Her
mission is to help you reach financial goals through a personal relationship
based on knowledge and advice, paired with financial planning.

Preal Haley

Photo by Kendra Lewis

 Q&A

What are your most popular
products or services?
General financial planning, investment
advice, income tax planning, retirement
planning, protection and insurance
solutions, estate planning, family
planning, and saving for education.

Who is your role model or mentor?
I admire what Suze Orman has done to
encourage others to own their financial destiny.

What do you CRAVE? In business? In life?
In both business and life, the time to
enjoy—and help others enjoy—more of
the journey, not just the destination.

RED DRESS STUDIOS

512.827.7733
reddressstudios.com, Twitter: @anaottman

Bold. Creative. Feminine.
Red Dress Studios helps women business owners build their confidence muscles.
Feminist, progressive women rock their small businesses via this customized,
tailored consulting program. Sessions address both the practical and emotional
aspects of entrepreneurship. With their clients' assistance, Red Dress Studios
simplifies, energizes, re-frames, and rocket launches. It's that simple.

Photo by Blue Lotus Photography

Ana Ottman

Q&A

What are your most popular
products or services?
The Red Dress Sessions. This is where
brilliant business ideas happen.

What or who inspired you to start your business?
The desire to create meaning
and purpose in my life.

How do you spend your free time?
Journaling, attending yoga class, being with
loved ones, and taking luxurious naps.

Where is your favorite place to
go with your girlfriends?
My living room to drink wine and
swap stories until the wee hours.

What do you CRAVE? In business? In life?
Simplicity, creativity, and fulfillment.

ROAR COACHING AND CONSULTING

301.483.3798
womenwhoroar.net, Twitter: @shessofierce

Creative. Innovative. Fierce.
Roar Coaching and Consulting is a personal branding agency. To empower women entrepreneurs, Roar gives them the tools they need to raise their business profile, position themselves as industry experts, and leverage their expertise to double their income while designing a dynamic living legacy in the process.

Photo by MoCoPhoto

Jennifer Ransaw Smith

 Q&A

What are your most popular products or services?
The six-month personal branding coaching intensive, the Undeniably Fierce home study system, and the Undeniably Fierce 12-week bootcamp.

What or who inspired you to start your business?
The little voice inside that told me it was time to stop playing small and to step up in a big, bold way.

Who is your role model or mentor?
Ali Brown, Fabienne Frederickson, and the new crop of business women who are currently redefining the old-school business model.

What do you CRAVE? In business? In life?
A life without regrets... infused with passion, purpose, and profits!

$ SIDELINE PREP

4206 Lavender Lane, Bowie, 703.582.8772
sidelineprep.com, Twitter: @sidelineprep

Spirited. Glamorous. Fun.
Sideline Prep is a consulting company providing one-on-one guidance, advice, coaching, and personal appearance consultations to individuals (both male and female) aspiring to become professional cheerleaders or dancers. They aim to please clients by giving them individualized and tailored attention to address all of their questions, concerns, and needs for the audition process. They have the "Inside Scoop to Professional Cheerleading & More!"

Photo by Washington Redskins Cheerleaders

Sooin Reese and
GeNienne Samuels

Q&A

What or who inspired you to start your business?
In our 10-plus years each of experience in professional cheerleading, we have answered millions of questions about auditions and have helped friends and strangers. We realized that there are a lot of unknowns about professional cheerleading/dancing that we can help answer.

People may be surprised to know...
All of our Sideline Prep Coaches are current and/or former professional cheerleaders with the NFL, NBA, NHL, MISL, AIFA. You name it... we know it!

Where is your favorite place to go with your girlfriends?
Out to eat or to a lounge to catch up. We are all going in different directions these days, so a low-key gathering hits the spot.

SINCERE PHOTOS

sincerephotos.com

Creative. Fun. Genuine.
Sincere Photos keeps the client's needs in mind at all times. Each photo shoot is done with care and precision, with the aim to capture a memory. Shoot locations are determined by the client.

Photo by Cedric Boyd

Kendra Lewis

 Q&A

People may be surprised to know...
Under no circumstances will I watch a scary movie!

What business mistake have you made that you will not repeat?
Forgetting to place my watermark on photo proofs.

How do you spend your free time?
I like to travel to new places whenever I can.

What is your indulgence?
I absolutely love chocolate and my guilty pleasure is *Gossip Girl*.

What do you CRAVE? In business? In life?
I crave great success in business and in life.

$ SVELTE

202.642.5517
svelte-emc.com, Twitter: @SVELTELLC

Innovative. Refined. Versatile.
SVELTE is a creative consulting and communications firm that specializes in large-scale fashion show production, visual and strategic brand development, and promotional/broadcast media for fashion and lifestyle brands. SVELTE is the parent company of fashion radio show "Fashion BS," fashion channel SVELTE Tv, and the production house responsible for Fashion Fights Poverty's annual benefit, named Washington's Top Fashion & Beauty Events by *BizBash Magazine* two years in a row (2008 & 2009).

 Q&A

Photo by Tim Coburn Photography

Elaine Mensah

What or who inspired you to start your business?
My love of Washington DC. I didn't want to move to pursue my dreams so I decided to create them.

People may be surprised to know...
I had no interest in fashion until my late teens. It shows you never know where life may lead.

How do you spend your free time?
Work/life balance is critical so I spend free time with family, friends, and my DVR.

Where is your favorite place to go with your girlfriends?
My girlfriends and I love to relax over a good meal and great ambiance so we enjoy Co Co. Sala and Oya.

THEGIRLFRIENDGROUP

571.252.9029
thegirlfriendgroup.ning.com, Twitter: @girlfriendgroup

Fresh. Dynamic. Powerful.
TheGirlfriendGroup is a global professional and social networking
community for women. Their motto is "Women helping women
in all aspects of life." They are a diverse, highly dynamic group
of women who aspire to network, share, and encourage.

Vanessa Maddox

Photo by Roger Maddox

 Q&A

**What are your most popular
products or services?**
We offer women a safe, secure venue to
make personal and business connections.

People may be surprised to know...
I started TheGirlfriendGroup with less than $100.

What or who inspired you to start your business?
My sister Valerie. She always inspired
me to go for it, no matter what.

What is your indulgence?
I love Crab Chips and pickle spears.

What do you CRAVE? In business? In life?
I crave prosperous relationships in
business, and loving, supportive,
healthy relationships in life.

$ UPTOWN GIRL VIP

866.230.3567
uptowngirlvip.com, Twitter: @uptowngirlent

Savvy. Influential. Chic.

Uptown Girl VIP offers an array of stylish freebies and exclusive deals on beauty, fashion, and lifestyle products and services, at the *insider* price. The program offers unbelievable deals on some of the most popular products and services, and helps members keep their fingers on the pulse of today's ever-changing lifestyle trends. Memberships make great gifts for birthdays, showers, and other special occasions.

Photo by Uptown Girl Entertainment, LLC

Bailey Sessoms

Q&A

What or who inspired you to start your business?
I enjoy lavish and beautiful things, but without the high price. I wanted to offer other women the same luxury.

People may be surprised to know...
I am not the CEO of Uptown Girl VIP, I'm only the name behind the brand.

What business mistake have you made that you will not repeat?
Compensating people who don't produce results.

What do you CRAVE? In business? In life?
Delivering a worthy product with charming customer service.

WARDROBE 180°

202.658.8037
wardrobe180.com, Twitter: @wardrobe180

Empowering. Creative. Savvy.
Jenn Bussell takes wardrobe styling to a new level by implementing comprehensive image turnaround strategies traditionally reserved for the boardroom. The Wardrobe 180° team combines their success at brand-building and extensive commercial and personal styling expertise with the shopping savvy of your best friend. The result is a 180-degree transformation and the emergence of a unique style that each client experiences from the inside... out.

Jenn Bussell

 Q&A

What or who inspired you to start your business?
My friends and former colleagues. For years, I'd been their go-to person to help them get dressed for special occasions. Seeing the joy on their faces when they looked in the mirror was worth its weight in gold.

Who is your role model or mentor?
Tim Gunn.

What business mistake have you made that you will not repeat?
The business plan for Wardrobe 180° has been sitting in a file folder circa 1999. The biggest mistake I've made was waiting 10 years to pursue my dream. Better late than never!

What do you CRAVE? In business? In life?
Happiness and a sense of fulfillment from helping others look and feel their very best.

A Guide to Our Manifest

 Abode Furniture, home improvement, and interior design

 Adorn Jewelry, eyewear, handbags, and accessories

 Children's Goods and services for babies, children, and parents

 Connect Networking, media, technology, and event services

 Details Gifts, books, small home accessories, florists, and stationery

 Enhance Beauty, wellness, spas, and fitness

 Escape Entertainment, travel, and leisure activities

 Pets Goods and services for pets and their owners

 Sip Savor Food and drink

 Style Clothing, shoes, and stylists

Featured Entreprenesses by Category

Featured Entreprenesses by Category (continued)

Featured Entreprenesses by Category (continued)

Intelligentsia by Category

Intelligentsia by Category (continued)

Entreprenesses by Neighborhood

Entreprenesses by Neighborhood (continued)

Entreprenesses by Neighborhood (continued)

Contributors

At CRAVE DC we believe in acknowledging, celebrating, and passionately supporting locally owned businesses and entrepreneurs. We are extremely grateful to all contributors for this publication.

Alison Turner
graphic designer
alisonjturner.com

Alison is a graphic designer, seamstress, and block printer from Seattle, who supports human rights and the local food movement. In her spare time she enjoys music, cooking, and being outside.

Amanda Buzard
lead designer and editor
amandabuzard.com

Amanda is a Seattle-based designer inspired by clean patterns and vintage design. She chases many creative and active pursuits in her spare time. Passions include Northwest travel, photography, dining out, and creating community.

Carrie Wicks
proofreader and copyeditor
linkedin.com/in/carriewicks

Carrie has been proofreading professionally for 14-plus years in mostly creative fields. When she's not proofreading or copyediting, she's reading, singing jazz, walking in the woods, or gardening.

Gunnar Larson
photographer
gunnarlarson.com

Gunnar, who is based out of DC and NYC, enjoys capturing time and space into an image that describes the essence of a person and the accomplishments in their life.

Kendra Lewis
photographer
sincerephotos.com

Sincere Photos keeps the client's needs in mind at all times. Each photo shoot is done with care and precision, with the aim to capture a memory. Shoot locations are determined by the client.

Lilla Kovacs
operations manager
lilla@thecravecompany.com

Lilla has been with CRAVE since 2005. As the operations manager, she ensures that everything runs like clockwork. She loves shoe shopping, traveling, art, and her MacBook.

Meredith Rizzo Photography
photographer
804.868.0821, meredithrizzo.com

Meredith is a Washington DC-based freelance photographer specializing in editorial, photojournalistic-style photography. With a passion for environmental portraiture, Meredith provides photography for events, weddings, publications, and nonprofit organizations.

Nicole Shema
project manager
nicole@thecravecompany.com

A Seattle native, Nicole is happy to be back in her city after graduating from the University of Oregon in 2009. Nicole has a passion for exploring new countries and cultures, and she loves discovering new places around Seattle with friends, running, shopping, and reading in coffee shops.

Patrick Onofre Photography
photographer
757.619.8032, patrickonofre.com
Twitter: @OnofreShoots

After working in restaurants for 10 years, this self-proclaimed "Light & Shadow Warrior" took on his creative side and conquers engagements, events, weddings, portraits, commercial and food photography.

Rhonda James
virtual assistant
thyrighthand.com

After eight years as a virtual assistant, Rhonda's wide-ranging familiarity with business practices, extensive administrative experience, and love of helping entrepreneurs all come together with great synergy in a new venture—designing custom back-office systems.

Sarah Clise
intern
monkeydomdia.wordpress.com
425.765.4650

Sarah graduated from Santa Clara University in 2008 and is now a freelance writer and social media maven. A Seattle native, she's been passionate about writing since she's been able to hold a pen and loves learning new words, traveling, and designing fingerless gloves.

Taline Yedibalian
intern
taline.Yedibalian@gmail.com

Having graduated Georgetown University in 2010, Taline is now pursuing a career in public relations in New York City. Her adventurous personality has led her all over the world, and she spends her free time hanging out on the beach with friends, skiing, and shopping.

Thank you to Milinda Jefferson and to our additional photographers, Eddie Paylor, Ezra Gregg, Jonathan Thorpe, Maggie Winters, Michael Kingsley, Nikole Charles, RL Campbell Photography, Sian Miranda Singh ÓFaoláin, and Troy of Ex Voto Studio.

About Our Company

The CRAVE company innovatively connects small business owners with the customers they crave. We bring together small business communities and fuel them with entrepreneurial know-how and fresh ideas—from business consulting to shopping fairs to new media. The CRAVE company knows what it takes to thrive in the modern marketplace. To find out more about CRAVE in your city, visit thecravecompany.com.

CRAVEparty®

What Do You Crave?
CRAVEparty is an exclusive, festive, glam-gal gathering of fun, entertainment, personal pampering, specialty shopping, sippin' and noshin', and just hanging with the girls.

CRAVE guides™

Style and Substance. Delivered.
CRAVEguides are the go-to resource for urban-minded women. We celebrate stylish entrepreneurs by showcasing the gutsiest, most creative, and interesting proprietors from cities all over the world.

CRAVEbusiness™

A Fresh Approach to Modern Business.
CRAVE business is all about making connections and sharing innovation. Our community is a diverse group of stylish, exciting, and driven entrepreneurs, and we create all kinds of ways for you to connect with each other.

Craving Savings

Get the savings you crave with the following participating entreprenesses—one time only!

10 percent off

- [ ] ADMK Jewelry
- [ ] Affinity Lab
- [ ] Angela Spicer Eco Make Up Artist
- [ ] Annalee's
- [ ] Art By Chocolate
- [ ] AudreyLynnJo LLC
- [ ] Bradley Wellness
- [ ] Carla David Design
- [ ] Chic Chocolate
- [ ] Chic Physique
- [ ] Color-Coded Organizing
- [ ] Creative Blog Solutions
- [ ] Current Boutique
- [ ] The Dandelion Patch
- [ ] Design Scheme Interiors, LLC
- [ ] Diva
- [ ] Dolce Studio Films
- [ ] Eco-Chic Body Care
- [ ] Eco-Coach
- [ ] EcoBliss Salon and Spa
- [ ] Holeco® life
- [ ] Indulge Mobile Spa
- [ ] Laura Lee Designs
- [ ] Metamorphosis
- [ ] Miss Pixie's
- [ ] My Body My Way
- [ ] Nicole Indelicato
- [ ] THE pearl
- [ ] Ra reDoes rooms
- [ ] Red Dress Studios
- [ ] Reston Limousine and Travel Service
- [ ] SAYA Originals

10 percent off (continued)

- [ ] Sissy Yates Designs
- [ ] Sisters & Such
- [ ] Spotted MP
- [ ] Studio-310
- [ ] TheGirlfriendGroup
- [ ] Tranquil Space

15 percent off

- [ ] Après Peau
- [ ] Bardangle Jewelry
- [ ] Compassionate Renegade
- [ ] Core Connection Lifestyle
- [ ] EnJoi Cupcakes
- [ ] Karin's Florist
- [ ] La Cuisine
- [ ] The Nest Egg
- [ ] Queen Bee Designs
- [ ] Quiet Mind Yoga
- [ ] Spiritual Essence
- [ ] The Still Point
- [ ] SVELTE
- [ ] Uptown Girl VIP

20 percent off

- [ ] Candy Beads Jewelry
- [ ] Catalyst Gourmet & Gifts
- [ ] Emily Kate Baby
- [ ] Fitness on the Run
- [ ] Frosting Bakeshop & Coffee Bar
- [ ] Impact Fitness DC
- [ ] The Point of it All
- [ ] Sideline Prep
- [ ] Stanton Gallery
- [ ] Twins Jazz Club

Craving Savings

20 percent off (continued)

- ☐ Urban Style Lab
- ☐ Valerianne
- ☐ VM Photography &
  Makeup Studio

30 percent off

- ☐ Blissliving Home
- ☐ Cynirje Culture by Design
- ☐ Dating Coach Jess McCann

50 percent off

- ☐ Celebrating You the Spa
- ☐ SAGE Interiors

Use code CRAVE for online discount if applicable.

Details of discounts may vary from business to business, so please call ahead. Neither the CRAVE company, CRAVE DC, nor the publisher shall be responsible for variations on discounts at individual businesses. This page may not be photocopied or otherwise duplicated.